The
CREATIVE
SOUND

SACRED MUSIC,
DANCE, AND SONG

TORKOM SARAYDARIAN

T.S.G. Publishing
Foundation, Inc.

The Creative Sound, Sacred Music, Dance and Song

© 1999 The Creative Trust

ISBN: 0-929874-68-4

Library of Congress Catalog Card Number: 99-71231

Printed in the United States of America

Cover Design:	*Tim Fisher* Cave Creek, Arizona
Printed by:	*Data Reproductions* Rochester Hills, Michigan
Published by:	T.S.G. Publishing Foundation, Inc. Post Office Box 7068 Cave Creek, Arizona 85327-7068 United States of America

Note: Meditations, visualizations, and other health information
are given as guidelines. They should be used with discretion and
after receiving professional advice.

Published from donations to the Torkom Saraydarian Book Publishing Fund.

Table of Contents

An Interview
with
Torkom Saraydarian

Torkom Saraydarian was born into a musical family. His Mother was an organist and pianist. His sisters were violinists, and his Father was a composer and a conductor of a small orchestra. Torkom was raised in an atmosphere of music and creativity. He attended almost all the rehearsals of his Father's orchestra.

Often he used to sit with students and listen to the lectures and rehearsals his Father was giving. Every week, and specifically on Saturday night, the family used to play sacred and folk music in the home.

Torkom did extensive studies in Middle Eastern and Far Eastern music. His specific interest was in sacred music, sung and played in monasteries, churches, and sacred brotherhoods.

He studied for many years on violin, cello, piano, guitar, mandolin, oud, and flute. In 1947 he became first violinist for the British Royal Air Force Orchestra. He has composed over 200 piano compositions and many songs. They not only give deep esthetic pleasure, but they also elevate and expand people's consciousness. About his music Torkom has said, "People are built by the music they listen to. In most cases the music they listen to crystallizes a pattern in their electromagnetic sphere. The intention of my music is to annihilate such crystallization and offer people opportunity to come in tune with the beauty that exists within them. My music brings health, happiness, and offers new channels of inspiration."

He says that most of his music is born through translating his visualizations into music. And it is true that you can almost see and hear in his music what he said he visualized in his mind.

Torkom Saraydarian gave a brief interview regarding his music.

Question: *When did you first become interested in music?*

ANSWER: My Father was a musician all his life in addition to being a pharmacist. When I was a child, he had a group of musicians who used to come to our home to play together two to three times a week. In the group there were three or four ouds, two violins, a clarinet, santur, drums, cello, guitar, and piano. They would play mostly Oriental, Persian, Turkish, Armenian, Kurdish, and Arabic music and sometimes western classical music. I would sit in a corner and with extreme delight literally absorb the melodies and rhythmic sounds.

Question: *When did you take your first music lesson?*

ANSWER: On Fridays and Saturdays, my Father used to teach music. For many years I did not have any formal music lessons, but I would sit with my Father's students and observe how he was teaching them and what they were doing. Then I would go to another room and practice by myself. I continued to learn this way between the ages of five and nine.

Question: *What was the first instrument you played?*

ANSWER: I think it was the oud. Then as my arms became longer, I started to play the violin, then the mandolin and drums. Around the age of fourteen, I started violin lessons and began to play the violin in little groups. At age seventeen I was interested in the piano, but at that time we did not have any instruments other than an oud and two violins in our home because of the genocide and the subsequent conditions, which presented severe financial difficulties.

During my twenties, I continued to play the violin seriously, and for several years I was concertmaster with the British Royal Air Force Orchestra in Jordan.

Question: *When did you start playing the piano?*

ANSWER: I began to play the piano when I was around forty-five years old. In addition, I began to teach myself the clarinet, the santur, and the cello. I noticed that each instrument could express something in me that others could not. When I play a variety of instruments periodically, I feel released and fulfilled.

Question: *Do you think that formal teaching in music could add something to your compositions?*

ANSWER: My answer is yes and no. On one hand, I am glad I was not pressured by the orthodox, classical, or traditional way of playing music. I think it would have some limiting effect on my creativity. It could hinder and mold the current of inspiration that flows out of my heart. I never wanted to imitate or follow the path that other composers have trodden. On the other hand, sometimes I feel that it would be marvelous if I had experience in orchestration because I feel that some of my piano compositions would make exceptional orchestral works.

Question: *What are your future plans?*

ANSWER: I have hundreds of pieces composed at this time, mostly for piano, and I want people to enjoy them. I hope to see them all published in sheet music and on recordings for future generations. I believe that I have made a breakthrough in the musical field, and I would like future musicians to know what I did and how I did it. Most of all, I want the world to hear this music.

Question: *How do you compose?*

ANSWER: My compositions are the translations of moments of inner experiences, states of consciousness, visualization, and identification with some of my life's dreams. During my composing, I try to use the notes as if they were colors in the air, with their specific shapes and hues. For example, I may create a rose in the air with the flow of the sound. My visualization is translated into notes to build that rose exactly as I see it in my vision.

Every piece for me is a formation of architectural and natural forms. If music cannot be built by vision, then there is something wrong with it.

I also create different scenarios. For example, I visualize high mountains, the moon, snow falling, and a little hut with a boy sitting near a fire. I visualize inner states of consciousness, and I create music corresponding to such states.

I generally receive my inspiration from inner states of consciousness or from outer events or scenarios that present some symbolic form of my inner states of beingness. For example, a river, a creek, a lake with birds, a waterfall, bamboo, or flowers are for me the symbolic manifestation of my inner states of beingness.

Question: *What are the things that inspire you most in your composing?*

ANSWER: I receive great inspiration from trees, flowers, oceans, lakes, canyons — in short, from Nature. I receive inspiration from artworks, such as the paintings of Nicholas Roerich and the poetry of Rabindranath Tagore. I also receive inspiration from fairy tales and legends and from those people who try to demonstrate a sacrificial life.

I want my music to reveal those states that words cannot express. For me, music is intuitional conversation, which tells me more about reality than any other symbol or word does.

The soul has many layers. Some composers and musicians speak to only one or two layers, but those who are in the flame can talk to all layers of your soul. This is where you feel ecstasy and complete fulfillment. This is the moment when transformation and transfiguration begin in your nature.

Composers talk through music. It is strange to note that some of them start sentences and do not finish them. Some repeat their half sentences without making any sense. Some start talking and then suddenly change the course of their talk and jump from one subject to another.

There are only a few who know how to *talk* and make sense from the beginning to the end, with emotion, thought, and vision.

Of course, there are many grades in talk. Some talk for the past; some for the present; some for the future. There are also those who speak like babies — only a few words and short sentences. Advanced composers talk to your heart, soul, and mind simultaneously, and their "speech" evokes all the beauty that is hidden within you.

Question: *How would you explain the effect of music upon others?*

ANSWER: If the music is of a high quality, it affects people as a fragrance does. It also purifies the space and establishes harmony. It may also heal on all levels. I remember the words my Father once said to a group of musicians, "Good music heals all your ills and makes you able to discover treasures within yourself."

Question: *About the music you have composed, how should we utilize it?*

ANSWER: Without attachment I recommend that you listen to my music. It is the only sounds purposefully created to destroy your crystallizations. If you have any crystallization physically, emotionally, and mentally, listen to this music one hour daily, and one week later you will not have those crystallizations. This music might initially "bug" you. Many people do not like it because their crystallizations fight against it. But give it one week and see what is happening to your consciousness. Sit quietly and listen to it. This way it penetrates into your aura, into your etheric, astral, and mental bodies. Do not listen to it while going to sleep. This would be hypnotic. Just read the commentaries on the songs. Then listen to the music. If you are sincerely listening, one week later you will want to listen to it more. This music will purify your whole system if you do hard labor to change yourself in the meantime.

A university professor once wrote, "I heard your obnoxious music and put it away. But later when I was divorcing my wife, I was looking for some music and your tape popped out. I listened to it into the early morning hours, crying as I listened. When I was finished, my consciousness was very expanded and beautiful. I went directly to my wife and asked her to listen to this music with me. We are now back together." This music creates transformation.

My music is a very powerful means to destroy crystallizations in your aura — etheric, astral, and mental crystallizations. Once your crystallizations are broken and dispersed from your aura, you have a great chance to build new behaviors, new kinds of responses, and new ways of thinking.

You must listen to the music in a very relaxed and focused way, absorbing every move of it with the intention to transform yourself, until you are able to memorize it. You must not be passive but conscious and awake while you are listening.

It is very important to understand that if you listen to this music while you want to keep your negative emotions in your heart, your hidden motives in your mind, and your jealousy in your bones, the music will amplify them and bring them to the surface. Many people turn into traitors and others fall into paths of crime and slander. This is similar to feeding yourself with vitalizing food and taking vitamins. You use the energy for what you are. You stimulate your vices if you have them, and you become the victim of your vices.

It is important that people do not overcharge themselves through meditation, reading, listening to my music, or eating extra food before they have a pure heart to use the energy for worthy purposes. Increasing the supply of energy works in positive or negative ways. People do not understand that to benefit from highly charged music they must have clean motives and life directions.

Once you decide to live for the service of light, love, and beauty, my music will take you on its wings and lead you to your spiritual destination.

Chapter 1

Foundations of Creativity

Creativity is a result of the circulation of energies when they pass through our etheric, emotional, and mental vehicles and purify them, regenerate them, and recreate them.

Energies are as necessary to our subtle bodies as they are necessary to our physical body. Through these energies our bodies regenerate and finer bodies are created. These energies not only bring the creative process into our etheric, astral, and mental bodies, but they also bring powers of new creative imagination, visualization, and higher and more subtle substance to be used to give form to the ideas and visions.

These energies in their totality are light energies, love energies, and willpower energies. Ideas seek manifestation through our etheric centers. Love seeks expression through our purified and organized astral centers. Will energy seeks manifestation through our unified and highly organized mental centers.

Ideas are currents of light energy emanated from human, planetary, and solar sources in the form of thoughtforms, inspirations, impressions, or merely currents of energies with specific direction.

The mechanisms of contact of these energies are our centers, the Antahkarana, the mental mechanism, astral, and etheric bodies. We need to register these energies, then assimilate them and express them through our creative activities, emotions, and thoughts to bring transformation or changes in the world.

Creativity is the fusion of energies with the matter of etheric, astral, and mental substance to make the *Plan* actualize and the *Purpose* be fulfilled.

Light energy comes to us through our throat center, from our Higher Self, from the knowledge petals, from Venus, the Pleiades, and Sirius, or from other constellations which operate under the Third Ray.

To repeat, higher energies of light come from those constellations which have the Third Ray. Also it comes from Venus. Venus is one of the great Centers of Light in the solar system. Another great center is the Pleiades, which provide light for all seven sacred planets. Then there is another greater light center which is called the Sun Sirius that also provides light.

If man is going to be creative, he must have light. He accumulates these lights and registers them from wherever he can due to his level of consciousness and beingness. He absorbs these lights, assimilates, and then circulates them throughout his system, bringing regeneration, unfoldment, and development in all his centers, especially in the etheric centers. Light works with the etheric body, with the centers of light in the astral body, such as the throat center, and with the knowledge petals of the mental body. We have a really organized mechanism! The Universe is an organized mechanism as well.

Your level determines your ability to receive, assimilate, and express light. If you are at the kindergarten level, you will not be able to receive light, assimilate it to a great extent, and express it. Not only is your development necessary but also your purification because there is danger in invoking light. When light comes as an energy, it destroys things which belong to darkness within your system. This destruction sometimes causes psychological upheavals. Some people go through trauma not because they are ignorant, not because they have no light, but because they have abundant light which they cannot handle. It is like a carburetor. It usually functions nicely, but if you put too much gas in it, it does not function because that carburetor is not built to assimilate that additional energy and use it creatively.

Purification is also important within your physical body, emotional body, and mental body. If light comes and hits your emotional system, it creates a neurosis, and that is what is happening to humanity. Millions of people are invoking light, "Let Light descend on earth." This is fantastic, but people are going crazy. Do we not need light? We need light. We need more light. We are not going to stop the inflow of the light, but we are going to purify ourselves so that we use the light creatively. Until your mechanism is ready, until your mechanism is purified, the energies you are receiving will give different results than you are expecting.

What are you actually doing? You are hooking your electrical system or machine into a plug that is loaded with energy. To assimilate these energies you are going to prepare your body, your emotions, and your mind. It is not hocus pocus artistry. That is why you can see in films, television, and in various programs millions of artistic expressions that are leading our nation and humanity into destruction. Why is this? Your creative forces are coming and manifesting negatively. If you have crime in your mind, the light is blowing that crime out of proportion and creating a script that is all violence, killing, and destruction.

If you observe what is happening in humanity, you will see how these energies are creating and destroying at the same time. If your physical, emotional, and mental bodies are beautiful, you are uplifted like a surfboard on the waves of human emotions, activities, and thoughts. You are always balanced, have equilibrium, and are creative.

These two kinds of people are increasing in humanity, and we are expecting or seeing that a final clash is inevitable.

The second energy is love energy. Love energy originates from your heart, from your Solar Angel. Love energy comes from all those constellations that have the Second Ray. It comes from the Hierarchy. It comes from Christ. It comes from those centers that are hooked into the creative currents of the Universe. The Son is the result of the Father and Mother, or Light and Power.

When this love energy comes within your system it really activates your emotional body, and if your emotional body is loaded with hatred, anger, fear, malice, revenge, jealousy, or treason, you have lots of trouble in your system. Not only your health suffers but also your relationships because love is related to human relationships, building a family, building groups, building society, and establishing within them right human relations. Right human relations is an expression of the manifestation of love energy.

You are going to be creative in the sense that you have a great vision within you. You are sensing that that vision is a part of the Hierarchical Plan, and you are going to actualize that vision through your light and through your love. But preparation is necessary so that when you are receiving energies, you do not pollute and distort the directions, the Purpose, the Plan that exist in each atom of the energy flow that is reaching you. The Great Teacher says that in the future great creative people are going to incarnate when the Fourth Ray starts to come to our globe. He says that today's masterpieces will seem like baby toys to the creative results of those people who really, scientifically, psychologically, esoterically prepared and understood the meaning and process of creativity.

The third energy is will energy. Every artist who really dedicates his life to creative activities must develop these three energies so that he balances light, love, and power. Where does this will energy come from? It comes first when your head center is stimulated and starts unfolding. It comes from the will center in the planet and solar system. Will energy awakens in your consciousness the feeling of your destination.

We have a phrase we use sometimes which says, "He is lost." Some people are lost, and we need to search for them and find them. We must be brave and daring to find them. When we find them, we must be careful that they are not contaminated.

Why are they lost? It is because there is not one single drop of will energy in their system. If you do not have a plan, if you do not have a goal, if you do not have purpose in your life, you are lost. You can have lots of love, lots of light, but use light and love for your own destruction. Until you find your purpose, you cannot find your direction.

What is the direction? Read *The Purpose of Life,* which gives the direction. Take that book and really dig into it. When the will energy comes, galvanizes, suddenly your light and love start functioning with the power — goal-fittingly, purposefully. You no longer exploit these energies to be rich, to be famous, to control people, to manipulate them through your own creativity.

I was watching television and a lady was talking about a film, for me the most obnoxious film ever created, and she said, "It had the greatest impact on our nation because it made one hundred twenty-seven million dollars in one month." Look at the measurement!

There are two ways to use these three energies. One way is that you accumulate these energies within your system and use them for all your selfish goals, plans, and interests, and you create more cleavages and more destruction because of your creativity. When your system is not clean and purified, these energies turn into poison. Let us say you have a stagnant pool and you bring the cleanest water and pour it into the stagnant pool. What difference does it make? The stagnant pool only becomes larger. That happens, exactly, in the creative process.

The second way to use these energies is that when you accumulate these rays within your etheric system: light, your mental system; love, your astral system; and willpower, in your higher mind, they organize, integrate, make inclusive and synthesize the higher mind, enabling it to stand the charge of the willpower. If you invoke willpower before you are ready mentally, it makes you berserk, nothing else. You become totally frustrated in your life. Actually, what happens is that when the energy of

Cosmic willpower prematurely hits you, you really start standing against your own light, against your own love, against your creativity. This is very scientific, and if you think about it you will see how many layers of meaning will be opened within your consciousness.

The first energy creates civilizations. Immediately when light comes, it creates competition. That competition creates groups running for their own interest. Then these groups clash together and bankrupt each other, and a third kind of group comes that has more love and power and synthesizes them. This is exactly what happens within yourself.

When these three energies are equally received, assimilated, and manifested in your system, you will see that something fantastic is happening. You are hooking yourself to these higher and higher sources in Cosmos and with these energies transmutation, transformation, and transfiguration are going on in your whole system. That is why we say that service and creativity are the means to transfiguration.

Every day we need purification. We are just a little lake, and if we have three pure currents coming to our pool, they are continuously taking away and cleaning the mess that is sitting on the surface of the inside of our pool. Your physical nature is purified through light, your emotional nature is purified through love, your mental mechanism is purified by willpower, and then this purification creates integrity.

Integrity is a scientific word. Integrity means that these three energies, simultaneously and in the same dosage, are circulating throughout your three bodies and fusing them together, transforming, transmuting them together, and eventually through these three energies and their circulation, something exceptional is happening. You are born anew. Something is born in you. Your spirit is coming into existence. Now you exist. Before you were not. How beautiful it is to know these things and slowly, slowly realize how, and for what, you are using your physical life.

You worked for fifty years. What did you do? You talked so much about love. Where is the result of your love? Do not tell me that there is so much love in the world. Where is the result? Still people are cutting each other's throats. People are watching and saying, "It is diplomacy. It is politics."

Light creates civilization, and love creates cultures. If you read the history of humanity, you will see that great cultures came at the moment of history when the Second Ray hit certain nations and opened their heart centers and that culture came in. No historian reads life like this. Historians are just recording who knifed whom, who destroyed whom, how many people attacked whom. They record how many nations occupied the territories of other nations and felt proud.

What is culture? Culture is the synthesis of the best books, the best arts, the best music, the best religions; all things that came into existence from the heart center and built the culture of humanity, the culture of nations. No one will cooperate with all those who are creating culture if his heart center is closed and, for the sake of his religion, nation, race, color, he manipulates and exploits other people. Until your heart center opens and has a chance to proceed from the etheric plane into the astral and mental and higher, you will be a cocoon in the etheric plane after you die. These things must be said.

What does the willpower do? Willpower, when it comes, immediately puts your physical, emotional, and mental mechanisms into order. What does this mean? It means that you synchronize your physical, emotional, and mental activities with the Plan of the Hierarchy, with "the Center where the Will of God is known." Now your existence has value. You are conscious; you know where you came from, where you are going, and how you are going. The will energy synthesizes, creates units, and shows them the destination. It integrates your bodies. Actually, when the First Ray starts to work, the involutionary tendencies of your body turn toward evolution. The entities which are forming your physical, emotional, and mental bodies, who are by nature involutionary, separative, materialistic, turn to the path of evolution.

Light brings lots of information into your mind; love teaches you how to use this information so that you create a decent world. Willpower creates beingness in you. You not only know, you not only act and lecture and write, **but you are.** You become something. Your beingness is related to your willpower. Until the willpower comes, all your plans are hypocritical. You cannot actualize them. Willpower actualizes your visions. It materializes your visions, brings into practical operation your visions, and here you can stand. Instead of just being a man who talks, a man who loves, you are a man who actualizes his dreams. That is creativity.

In all your creativity, whether you are writing poems, books, creating music, architecture, etc., you are going to work with one purpose. Think how you can circulate all this energy so that the result of this activity brings happiness, success, prosperity, and enlightenment for all humanity. In this light, watch your television, read your books, and look at paintings, especially those where the paint is thrown on the canvas and sold for three thousand dollars. I visited a university where I was proudly shown a painting, 10 feet by 12 feet, on one of the university walls. The Dean said, "We bought this for eighteen thousand dollars." I looked at the painting and said, "Trash!"

What was the painting? It was the expression of an hallucinogenic, hypnotized, totally dreaming mind who did not understand where he stood or where he was going. There was no purpose in his life. He was throwing out whatever he was so that people could see what trash he was. You cannot build a house by throwing cement here, lumber there, the window here, the door there!

Creativity is not limited only to one field; all seven fields are creative. Wherever a person is he or she can be creative. Creativity has two branches:

1. To draw personal benefit from the creativity of these three forces — light, love, and will

2. To be creative for the sake of providing for the actualization of the Plan

In the first case, the evolution of the man does not proceed. His labor creates those karmic seeds which eventually destroy the selfish and self-interested person who manifests these three forces for his personal benefit, or his labor tries to knock down those who belong to the second category.

In the second case, the three forces purify and transform the vehicles of the creative worker to a higher and higher degree, enabling the person to penetrate into a higher plane of existence.

Be creative in your political life, in your educational field, in your communications and relationships, in your arts, sciences, religious field, and also be creative in your financial field.

Creativity is a dynamic power which

1. Expands your consciousness and cleans crystallizations and fanaticism

2. Expands the field of your service

Try to be creative in your field. Bring new light, new love, new purpose into your field, but dedicate all the results to the service of the Hierarchy.

Q&A

Question: *You were talking about the sources of light coming from constellations. Can you explain this further?*

ANSWER: Constellations that have Third Ray energy are the sources of light. Third Ray energy is always related to light. It is the Holy Spirit, psychic energy, or it is the World Mother in symbolic ways. We have these sources within us. One source within us is the throat center, also the petals around the Lotus related to knowledge, the light petals. Also, light comes from higher sources in space. If you are really creative, suddenly you will see that light, inspiration, and impressions are coming from a source you did not know about. This is not mediumship. Inspiration is not mediumship. Impressions are not mediumship. Revelations are not mediumship. It is a pure light that comes and hits the seeds within you and makes them to flower. The source did not decide what you are going to do with that energy. It is the seeds that you have that decide what will be the expressions of these energies. If you are a tomato seed, the light will come and make you a tomato plant. If you are a cabbage seed, you will be a good cabbage. If you are a rose bush, you will grow many roses. There is no Divine dictatorship that says everyone must produce cabbages.

But the sources of your inspirations and creative forces are not limited to your make-up, to what is in your body, in your emotions, in your mind. We can put jumper cables from constellation to constellation and bring their civilization and culture and beingness here. When a Great One comes, He brings a powerful stream of Light and Love and Beauty. It is not only coming from your head. You are becoming a radio station to broadcast the things you are receiving from space.

People think that space is empty. Space is all electromagnetic centers. These walls and the halls of this Temple are a center, and let us say it is built of condensed, materialized energy. But there are forms that are not yet materialized. They are electrical whirlpools, centers with thousands of petals, and each petal is connected with other universal centers. It is a matter of establishing a conscious link with these sources and transcending your lower level into the divine level. That is the destination. You are going to be creative.

What does it mean to be creative? To be creative means to be the co-workers of the Divinity Who brought all these things into manifestation. It has not ended yet. We are branches, leaves, and flowers in that Divinity and carrying on His creativity. You are a part of that creativity only if you consciously realize that you are a part of that process of creativity. You are not a money-making machine only. Make that money. Use that money for Hierarchy. Change humanity. Help all those who are working for light and love and beauty. This subject involves all the creativity of the Universe. Broadcast these things through other minds and say, "This life I am living is really purposeless, planless, goalless, wandering into darkness. I am going to come to my senses and save my etheric energies, emotional energies, mental energies. I am going to purify them and organize them so that I receive higher energies and become at least a transmitter in the huge machine of divine construction.

Question: *What makes a center open prematurely?*

ANSWER: It is electromagnetic short waves, the exposure of your brain to radioactivity, and trying to invoke more than you can use. For example, when you eat more than your stomach can digest, you take in lots of energy, but you also kill your stomach. You are going to purify yourself and organize yourself to be able to be a greater receiver.

Recently a man sent me a very complicated article from the Kalachakra Teaching. For one minute I felt so happy, as I understood it. "You know," I thought, "I wish everyone could understand this article."

You are going to make efforts. No one can help you. Where are you? What do you want us to do? Do you want us to open your mouth and put the book in? It is not going to go that way. Why are you ignoring and denying your evolution? That is what we must ask each other. Sometimes think and ask, "Why did I lose this day? What happened to those people lying under crosses in cemeteries is going to happen to me. Do I have a little time to shape myself?" That is the whole problem.

Question: *I am understanding that for mankind to evolve, mankind must have a changing heart in order to utilize that light. I am seeing so many different things. In some cities people are trying to get leaders to come and talk to the gangs.*

ANSWER: I really understand what you are saying. I really appreciate your heart because my heart also cries when I see what is happening. In large cities it is not a matter of talking with gangs. You must create right conditions, right education from the beginning, love, and purpose. Some classes have been started in a few places and little children are talking about how to handle problems with nonviolence. Look what is happening. I was thinking for many, many years, "God, why didn't you send me to the United States to take birth but instead You sent me to monasteries?" Later, I was so thankful that He did not send me here first, because for twenty-four years while I was secluded in the monasteries I had a chance to be myself and a chance to educate myself. This is not the case with children now. Let us prepare the atmosphere for children, a beautiful atmosphere, with the right teachers.

There is very, very good advice in the Bible where it says, "Whatever you sow, you will reap." Do not hate and condemn the fruits, the results, when you yourself put the seeds of corruption in the nation's consciousness. This is what we are going to pay attention to.

Chapter 2

Music and Sound

Sound is the source of all that exists in the Universe. Each atom, each form on any level is composed of sound.

The Ageless Wisdom teaches that all communication between created forms is based on sound, sound that is audible and sound that is inaudible. Sound manifests also as light and as energy.

Sound initially radiated seven energy currents which are called the Seven Rays. Each Ray is a note. Each note, or Ray, creates a plan. We are told that the continuity of sound brought into existence seven Cosmic Planes. Each Plane is becoming an octave with seven notes.

The human being in his own form is an embodiment of seven and forty-nine notes. The human soul, as an individualized note, uses his seven notes to relate with the Universe and with the forms in the Universe. The nature of the human being's relation with the Universe and Its forms is conditioned by the level of his consciousness, by the level of his evolution. Due to his relative evolution, the human soul uses his bodies sometimes according to the laws of Nature, sometimes against the laws of Nature. Every time he uses his bodies against the laws of Nature, he hurts his bodies and creates sickness and disease.

Wounds caused by acting against the natural laws accumulate life after life, complicating the health situation of the person not only on the physical plane but also on the emotional and mental planes.

Throughout ages people tried to heal the human being with many, many methods, with success and failure. Nature has not yet revealed the real method by which eventually all diseases will be healed, starting from the mental plane to the astral, etheric, and physical planes.

The secret of healing exists in sound, and Nature releases sound at various times that brings massive healing to people. For example, we have the sound of winds, hurricanes, tornadoes; the sound of ocean waves, the roar of volcanoes; the sound of massive fires, the sound of earthquakes, the sound of various kinds of natural destruction; the sound of waterfalls, rivers, creeks, rain on the roof; the sounds of natural explosions, such as thunder; the sounds of animals, birds, leaves, bushes, trees. If a scientific study is done about natural sound, it is very probable that scientists will discover the healing effects of sound on human ailments.

The vegetable kingdom and the animal kingdom are equipped with "ears" that surpass the capacity of the physical ear of the human kingdom. If enough study is carried out on the relations of these kingdoms to the sounds of Nature, it will be revealed that the vegetable and animal kingdoms are controlled and related to each other by special ultrasonic and infrasonic currents.

Big animals, like elephants and others, use ultrasonic sound to converse with each other over as much as one thousand miles of distance. But the most important point is that they follow the guidance of Nature in receiving Nature's direction expressed through various sounds. Also, they help themselves by carrying their bodies close to the source of those sounds that have special characteristics to heal them.

A horse not only responds to the natural sounds by its own sound, but it also has ultrasonic communication with Nature. A horse even hears the sound of human emotion and human thought. Those who have experience with horses may understand that horses "feel" their emotions and "hear" the sound of their thoughts.

All existence "lives, moves, and exists" in an Ocean of Sound. The Ageless Wisdom says that the AUM is that sound which sustains the existence of the Universe. If AUM stops sounding in space, the whole existence will disappear as a shadow.

In scientific circles it is not known that all human senses are threefold. We have, for example, physical ears, emotional ears, and mental ears. Throughout thousands of years some people were experienced in hearing astral and mental sounds, but science had no interest in such important experiences.

Animals have two ears: physical and astral. It is mostly their astral ears that hear ultrasonic and infrasonic vibrations.

We have also three eyes. There are eyes that see a physical form, but there are eyes that can see astral and mental forms. Science did not yet investigate such powers. The same holds true for the other senses.

When the consciousness of man passes into the monadic level, man uses one sense with seven spirals. This one sense synthesizes all seven senses. Each human being is destined to have such a sense during his evolution.

People's emotions and thoughts, whether negative or positive, are sound waves that reach their targets and effect them. Many physical, emotional, and mental disorders of people are the result of such contacts. They affect the health of our body, emotional moods, and mental attitudes. If they are persistent they can create health, happiness, and creativity or depression, pessimism, and diseases.

People's health is conditioned by the sounds they hear and by the notes they speak. Living in certain places and hearing different sounds change their health condition, for better or worse. The absence of certain notes develops certain sicknesses. Repetition of certain notes brings the same effect. Notes are living energies.

Colors are notes. Seeing or visualizing colors will change the chemistry of our bodies. The seven geometrical forms are seven chemical elements. The geometry of buildings and landscapes affects us, as sound does, as color does. Wrong combinations of sound, color, and form produce negative effects on our bodies.

Scientific living will start when all the above is understood by specialists.

What we know about the effect of sound, color, and form is very fragmentary. The history of humanity must be written in relation to sound, color, and form and to the resultant culture, civilization, and decay. These three factors hold the key to survival or degeneration.

In the future, the leaders of humanity will be equipped with the knowledge of sound, color, and form. Maybe they will be composers, painters, and architects, and they will use their talents to lead humanity toward mental, emotional, and physical health.

The human race will slowly compile all experiences and wisdom about the effects of sound, color, and form and develop the pure science of survival, right human relations, and creativity.

Nature tries to heal itself — its mineral, vegetable, animal, and human kingdoms — through sound. For example, the roar of a volcano has a very healing effect. It revitalizes the Nature — elemental, vegetable, animal, and human kingdoms — and brings various cures that are related to the mental, emotional, and physical worlds.

A flood cures different ills. A waterfall cures still other ills. Fire cures still other ills. The songs of birds are effective for various kinds of ills. If a scientific study is carried out on what the effects of various sounds are, especially on human nature, amazing revelations will be found.

Man, in recording all natural sounds and duplicating them when needed, can perform miracles. Wind passing through the needles of pine trees or deodars have a special effect on certain diseases. Such effects scientifically must be recorded and eventually used to heal corresponding illnesses.

Nature heals itself if man does not disturb the sound of Nature through his machinery, war games, bombs, and mechanical destruction. On one hand we have the natural, healing sounds. On the other hand we have the polluting, destroying sounds created by the dry human brain. If people want to survive, they must eventually eliminate the noise of the mechanical sounds and search for shelter within the natural sounds.

One must not be surprised, when in the future, special hospitals are built near waterfalls to heal certain diseases or sick people are transferred near active volcanoes or doctors prescribe certain sounds for certain diseases.

The evolution of sound is already gaining momentum, but it is mostly related to music and mechanical notes.

The treasury lies in natural sounds and their scientific effect on human psychology, the physical body, even in the human spiritual orientation.

In the future, scientific research will be carried out to prove that various nations, even states or groups, are shaped by the sound prevalent in their area.

Chapter 3

How I Compose Music

My compositions are built upon certain visualizations. Before I compose a piece of music, I visualize, for example, a lily near a lake reflected in the cool, calm water. Then I visualize a deer drinking water, and the concentric circles it makes on the surface of the water. This is my framework, which contains, of course, the trees, the rocks, the vegetation, and the lake with ripples upon it.

The second phase of composition deals with the feelings of the lily and the deer, the water and the trees. This makes the work a living event.

The third phase of composition deals with the symbology of the lily and the deer and the concentric waves. It is this symbology that evokes certain ideas, thoughts, and intuitive flashes from my higher realms and adds a new charge to the framework.

The fourth phase of composition is to translate these ideas, feelings, and symbols into music in such a way that they subliminally convey to the listener my feelings, ideas, and vision.

During the creation of the composition, I use the framework, the feelings, and the ideas presented by the symbols through my visualization and, in the meantime, try to translate my visualization into music.

I feel that as I proceed in such a labor, the outer and the inner parts of the symbols and meanings come closer to each other and I feel unified within myself.

Musical composition and performance is a unique opportunity to synthesize the subjective and the objective natures of our being. We thus eliminate cleavages existing in our psyche and let the creative current circulate within us without meeting any hindrances.

Creativity in music must be progressive so that gradually higher levels of our being are called out and fused with the objective side of our nature.

It is essential that we transform our lower nature into light and also make the light of our higher nature operate through the transformed mechanism on the physical plane without losing its magnitude and magnanimity.

In essence, all forms and their relationships with each other are nothing else but musical phenomena.

All forms, symbols, and ideas are condensations of musical notes. As ice melts to become water, so when any form melts away, it turns into sound, into a note.

The task of the musical genius will be to "hear" the notes of forms, symbols, feelings, and ideas, and translate them through the musical instrument. When such a task is a success, then the composer will realize that he himself is a combination of sounds, and his duty is to compose a symphony through these sounds, and thus unify or synthesize all his nature with the inaudible music of the Universe.

It is possible that one sits down and plays beautiful music in an "inspired" moment, and if we analyze this "inspired" moment, we will possibly find that it is a moment of tuning in between the outer circumstances or experiences and the inner aspirations, ideas, or visions formed around a symbol that was keyed in to the outer circumstance.

Often outer symbols are like keys in a computer that put a whole event or impression into action.

All creation and every form carries within itself the AUM. This is a symbol which refers to the creative chord existing in each form.

Disintegration of any form is the departure of the AUM.

Human consciousness can release the creative melody in each form or symbol that Nature created and compose a symphony, adding on it the melodies and rhythms found in his Chalice.

As the greater composers and musicians come to earth, they will compose such music which will literally

• Heal people
• Transform their nature
• Link them to their higher nature

Even it will be possible that such music will create conscious communications with the Higher Worlds.

Humanity will slowly realize that it is through sound that all beings and all forms in existence can communicate with each other.

As communication becomes conscious and involves higher and higher levels, the symphony of the Cosmos will emerge.

Chapter 4

Creativity of the Musical Mind

Music has many sides. The first two are contact and translation. Contact is the outer impact to your ears and brain. This can be pleasant or unpleasant according to the conditioning of the etheric centers. But by translation you can control the negative impact or enrich the positive impact.

For example, for one hour you hear the drum and you think, "This is boring; this is giving me a headache," but then you use your creative imagination and visualize a dance to the rhythm of the drum. The negativity disappears because of your translation. You not only create a dance but also a melody and music by using different notes between the beats or at the intervals of the beats.

Music has also an outer force which is the force of the musician — his body, his throat, etc. Reading the notes and playing the music add another dimension to music. The spirit you put into the music is also a dimension. The spirit is your dream, vision, enthusiasm, love, joy, and compassion. When music is played with its own notes and these inner dynamics are added, it is a different piece of music.

Most musicians only play the notes. Very few musicians play the notes and charge the music with their spirit. There are musical compositions which affect millions, raising them into ecstasy and joy. There are musical pieces which bring transformation in the nature of the listeners.

Every genius musician plays his music or sings for the sake of the music — in order to give a spiritual message to humanity. He never worries about the money, but money pours in. If he turns greedy because of the money, you can see the decline of his art.

Those who say that musicians do not make money prove that they were not musicians sent with a message to earth. Such people are merchants who create music only if they are paid. Usually such people do not succeed.

There is something divine in music, but you can betray the divinity in music.

Music is just like the urge to worship. It is there to create devotion, dedication, ecstasy, sublimity, and transformation. The music that does not serve its ideal is a prostituted music — which can contaminate millions and bring in degeneration.

Of course, to live in the true standards of music needs courage, daring, and long years of preparation.

Impact is another factor in music. It can be dealt with in four phases.

1. There is a physical impact, in which your physical body is in rhythm and harmony with the music, and you even have involuntary movements that bring you pleasure.

2. There is an emotional impact, which emotionally moves you. You are excited, you cry, you fall into many kinds of moods — exaltation, depression, or imaginations.

3. There is a mental impact, which makes you think, visualize, plan. It is very interesting that when the impact is mental, the mental body plans for the future or digs into past events.

4. Above these three impacts there may be a spiritual impact, which is a transformational impact. Because of the music, you leave behind certain things in your character and aspire to new virtues. Sometimes your whole character is transformed in the music when it hits your spiritual nature, the human soul, or the Intuition. Many great decisions are taken, and new ways of creativity are found under the spiritual impact of the music. Such music must originate from self-actualized people, not from merchants of music, in order to affect

your spiritual nature, and you must be advanced enough to receive such an impact.

Many musicians play the music with the force generated by their physical body. Others play exactly what the notes say. This is a mechanical way of rendering the music. Others translate the notes into their emotions, their thoughts, their dreams and visions, or they translate it through their future aspirations.

Still others use the notes as guidelines, but they soar above the notes and use the music to contact people's souls or spirit. This opens a challenge to those who are on the creative path, on the path of transformational labor.

In the Ageless Wisdom we are told, "We must remember." I thought this was an exoteric order, that we must remember the wisdom given by our Teachers, books, events, etc.

Then one day I had an experience. A light hit my mind and disappeared instantaneously. I asked, "What was that idea, that impression?" It was so quick. I noticed that it was an impact which I must remember. So I went into deep contemplation for a few hours, and *I remembered.* As I remembered, it unfolded into a book. A one second impact of the Ray of Light turned into a book, unfolding chapter after chapter in logical sequence.

Such moments come like falling stars, but they are within you. Remember them. Bring them out into your consciousness. Remember the seconds when you are caught in one moment of beauty, ecstasy, transformation and dig them out. Do not let them go; they are messages from the Higher Worlds.

If you start remembering, you will establish contact with these sources and enrich your life. After that you will be able to remember your Self.

Most of us remember world or life events. We are nothing but bodies, emotions, thoughts, not that deeper awareness unit that is the core of our being.

When you remember every moment that you are the Self — then you will start walking the path of Immortality.

Real music is the result of remembering the impressions and impacts given to you by Higher Worlds.

Chapter 5

Music and Ideas

Music is the manifestation of an idea through sound. We can receive an idea when we contact higher sources of inspiration within us, on the planet, or in space. An idea is relative to the source; the higher the source, the greater the idea.

When you register an idea and visualize a way to manifest it through sound, you create music. It is the idea that creates the melody, rhythm, harmony, and so on.

Many pieces of music do not have an idea behind them. If there is no idea in the succession of sound, there exists no music but only noise. In the same way there can be a combination of words, but with no idea there is no sentence and no meaning.

The origin of music must be an idea. For example, let us say you are inspired by the idea of renunciation.

You visualize the progressive movement and unfoldment of the idea; you feel and sense each phase of it. Then you create its vehicle of manifestation through sound. Thus, the idea creates or evokes mental response, emotional response, and sensory response.

If the composer is really inspired with the idea, feels it, and fuses it with his aspiration and thoughts, you will hear the idea in the music. Not only will you hear the idea, but you will feel that, for example, the music on renunciation is awakening a deep aspiration in you toward renunciation, and you are going through a certain transformation within your vehicles that will enable you to bring the idea of renunciation into actualization.

The expression of the sound or the music will be charged with meaning and feeling. The idea will build its rhythm and melody in the process of expression. Sometimes your technique and knowledge become an obstacle, if they are crystallized and exist for their own interest. Sometimes your technique and knowledge of music assist the birth of the idea, if they have not yet turned into hindrances.

If there is no idea behind the music, you have sound and notes but no music.

If the idea is coming from higher sources, it is charged by a tremendous amount of energy with its own frequency and direction.

The greatest help for the manifestation of the idea is the treasury of your Chalice. The Chalice should contain the needed vehicle of manifestation. It is the treasury of the Chalice that determines the color or the type of art, as well as the idea that is going to be chosen for manifestation.

True music is the flow of an idea, the flow of energy. Each piece of music radiates the energy of an idea.

Some ideas can only find a response in the etheric plane; the etheric plane sets the rhythm. Some ideas can manifest through emotional substance; emotions give the idea the fire of feeling. Some ideas can also manifest through the mental substance; a mental response is created, and the idea becomes charged with meaning. If the receiver of the idea is of a higher order, the idea also equips itself with a great and inclusive vision.

Each substance with which the idea is equipped radiates a particular form of energy. If the energies are combined in harmony, you have a piece of music that serves as a bridge between you and the originating source of the idea. The composer takes the seeds of ideas from the originating sources and gives them back to the sources as bloomed flowers.

The energy of the idea has many tasks. It creates, harmonizes, purifies, transforms, heals, organizes, makes breakthroughs, and builds communication lines to the originating sources.

If there is no idea, there is no energy; but there is the force of the sound. This force is the flow of illusions, glamors, and changing moods. When glamors, illusions, urges, and drives are translated into sound, they do not present the coherency of an idea. They are like sentences which do not make sense; they have the power of individual words, but not the power of a sentence. There is hallucination in the musical expressions, and they do not make sense. Hallucination has no coherency of meaning. You cannot translate a meaning out of it, but you feel the disturbance in the originating source.

It is the idea that gives to the succession of notes meaning, significance, and its manifested energy. If there is no idea behind the "music," the music is like a drunken man whose conversations and behavior translate no coherent meaning and have no destination.

The idea in music is the soul of the music; it makes it alive and purposeful. Music that has no soul has no future, although it may continue to exist as a disturbing factor.

Music can be the translation of past memories or the translation of present interests, urges, drives, or pleasures. It can also be the translation of the future or of a distant vision.

There is also music that bridges the future and past memories, translating the past memories as future visions and the future as the vision of past experiences. Such music carries a great amount of emotion and a power of transformation.

There are also various kinds of music originating from many force fields. Such music can originate from hatred, fear, anger, greed, jealousy, revenge, or lust. It can use your lower etheric centers to draw substance out of them.

There is music that translates your past pleasures, disappointments, failures, and successes, but without the light of the future.

There is music that can be an expression of vanity, pride, separatism, and ego.

There is music that disturbs your head centers, creates confusion and uncontrolled urges and drives, and leads you into hypnotic trance or toward suicide and irresponsibility. Such music makes you lose your striving, your focus, and your sense of responsibility and develop dependency.

People never think that most of our social problems are the result of bad music, music originating from lower sources.

There is music that rings in your ears and body but leads you into confusion, as a friend who speaks and speaks but does not make sense.

Of course, it is possible to take meaningless music and superimpose upon it certain meaningful phrases, sometimes high-sounding phrases, that make you swallow the aberrations of the sound. Many disturbing influences are transmitted to the public as music, packed in high-sounding phrases.

Such a technique not only creates disturbances in the mechanism of the mind but also a great confusion in the thinking. The meaningful phrases and the unmeaningful, low-grade music influence different parts of your nature and make them fight against each other.

There is also music that is hypnotic. In hypnotic music there are many techniques used: short suggestions, contradictory statements, repetition, confusion, monotony, forceful impact, and so on. Through such music many post-hypnotic suggestions are transmitted or evoked. Sometimes such music is used politically, for self-interest, for business, or directly for crimes.

There is also music that releases or evokes your aggressive urges and drives, charges them with emotion, involves the mind, and forces you to attack, possess, and obsess. Most of the wars, revolutions, social disorders, and crimes do not originate from idealistic flights; they have their origin in bad music, which is either prepared intentionally or is the natural manifestation of the composer. The prevalent music of the youth determines the future of the nation and the world.

No one has contemplated yet on how to create a law about music, or about art in general, as a factor that influences the life of people. Of course, such a law will turn into a mechanism of suppression in the hands of those who lack understanding, the power of evaluation, and are stuck with their past values.

The ancients knew the effect of sound, especially on advanced people, and they built pyramids to insulate the neophyte from all kinds of sound and put his soul in relation with Higher Worlds. But now we are exposed to all kinds of short and long waves, radiations that carry mixed, polluted, disturbing, and distorting influences to our homes, offices, and sanctuaries.

Man can destroy himself by misusing sound waves. But as the intelligentsia realize the influence of music upon the masses, they will create proper scientific methods and apparatuses to judge the value of music and of art in general. Every art object and every piece of music has various emanations and influences. Like a kind of spectroscope, the apparatuses they will create will be able to measure such emanations. These apparatuses will tell scientists if the music or art object is constructive and goal-fitting or destructive, diffusive, and disturbing.

The first steps will be taken through observation. Children and students will be observed under the influence of music. Their health and emotional and mental waves will be measured and compared. Once this process is established, teachers will teach the basics of the mechanics of art and prepare causes and conditions to put artists in contact with higher sources of inspiration.

A law can only be established on scientific facts or on pure experiences. Without this foundation, a law is nothing but an imposition. Eventually one law is going to be strictly observed: that no one has the right to disturb his neighbor at any time whatsoever. This law will be observed in restaurants, in other public places, at the seashore, and in the mountains. People will not dare to bring their music machines and disturb the peace of any human being.

Of course, similar laws are already formulated, but they are neither enforced nor observed by the majority of citizens. One can even hear the neighbor's television or radio. Consideration for others will be practiced when people respect each other and understand the power of music.

It is not enough for a composer to contact a great idea; it is also important to discover the focus of his consciousness. Wherever your focus of consciousness is, from that focus your idea will be translated and your expression will carry either the energy of your focus or its contamination. You can know the level of the focus of a composer by the effects his music has on the public. If the youth are stimulated in their sexual activities beyond control, if they are inclined to crime, irresponsible actions, drugs, and prostitution after listening to certain music, then you will know from what level or focus that music was originated.

The influence of music must be observed on physical health conditions, on emotional reactions, on family and social relationships, on mental interests and abilities, on striving or failures, on motivations. The effects in all these areas will clearly indicate the condition and level of the source of the music.

Every piece of music carries with it the quality of the composer. An artist who is involved in alcohol, drugs, prostitution, and crimes can contaminate masses of people through his music. If a composer is living in hallucinations, his music will carry out his hallucinations.

Once a young lady invited me to her studio to see the "masterpiece painting" she had created the night before in her inspiration. After looking at the painting I said, "How did you do this?"

She sat on the chair, looked at her painting with pitiful admiration, and said, "Last night, I found a drug formula and mixed a few drugs and took them. I felt myself elevated into heaven, and I took the brush and painted."

She had done a good job! She had taken the paint and scattered it not only on the canvas but also on the walls and curtains!

"Tell me," she asked, "do you like it?"

"It will make no difference to you whether I like it or hate it."

There are millions of pieces of music broadcast from radios, tapes, and televisions, as well as performed live, that are creating in the public such a state of mind, and the public is not even aware of it.

When music is the expression of hallucinations, lust, crime, drugs, and irresponsibility, it will carry to the public the elements of hallucination, lust, crime, drugs, and irresponsibility found in the artist, like a source of contamination. If the music is fused with gonorrhea, syphilis, anger, resentment, and confusion, people will be infected because their centers and nervous systems will respond to that frequency and begin to manifest the same characteristics and symptoms of the artist.

From whichever center a piece of music originates, the corresponding center of the listener will gradually synchronize its vibrations to the originating center. This is how contamination occurs. Thus, music is responsible for what a man is, what a nation is, and what humanity is.

Even animals have instinctive discrimination. In a certain place, two elephants were chained and nearby a band of musicians began to play acid rock music. These elephants, who used to perform in circuses with certain music, broke their chains, broke down the fences, and began to run away from the music. The incident was reported in a local paper as a funny event. What a great scientific labor is needed to understand the mechanics of such an event!

In the future, thinkers will find out how music can create certain illnesses and diseases in certain parts of the body. They will be able to trace the source of illness to the music the person listened to for years, or throughout his lives.

Our body is built on the principle of sound expressed as notes,[1] as vibration, as frequency. Flowers, bushes, and trees are built on the same principle. The sound waves create either harmony or disturbances in them. For example, because you were hearing certain kinds of music, you developed liver problems or kidney problems or heart problems or skin problems. Or because of the music you heard, you have the best health possible.

People worry only about nuclear radiation, but they never think that music is a form of radiation. Sound

---

1. Notes are the words of sound.

bombards the body, the brain, and the glands and creates certain effects.

The notes in music are chemical elements of sound. A good musician is a good chemist who knows when to use what element and in what proportion. These chemical compounds can change the elements in your body by increasing, decreasing, or totally eliminating them. These chemical changes in your body create changes in your psychology, behavior, relationship, thinking, feeling, talking, and so on.

When you are listening to music, you must know that you are absorbing chemical elements into your system. We do not yet have an apparatus to convince the "blind" about these facts, but steady observation and experiences with music will not leave any doubt in people's minds about chemical changes.

Sound controls the function of cells and neurons, and the chemical reactions and secretions of the glands. Eventually scientists will prove that both the mentally impaired and the genius are the products of agelong bombardment by certain music.

One may ask, if music must be listened to for an ideal condition of the body, emotions, and mind, then how can we help people who live in violent psychological conditions in asylums? The answer is that people in asylums must not listen to music, but they must listen to the music of waterfalls, rivers, forests, and thunder. Also, rhythmic drums can have a great healing influence on them, if the rhythmic patterns are created by a sensitive composer.

The music of a great composer passes through various changes in those who listen to it and in those who play it. If the performer is closely fused with the consciousness of the composer and does not carry disturbing emotions and thoughts against him, and if he has enough practice and skill, and if he is experienced in the art of listening, then he can transmit the initial currents of the composer with a high level of accuracy. Unfortunately, not too many performers can do this. They can only mechanically reproduce the music without the spirit of the composer.

If the composer plays his own music, then you have all possible shades and colors of thought and emotions that he put in his music. Beyond this, there should be electricity in the music. This electricity is transmitted by the composer into his music at the moment of his contact with sources of inspiration in higher spheres.

Distortion of the original music carries heavy consequences for the performer and for the audience.

Good music, or music that is composed by an artist who is in contact with higher sources of inspiration and is able to transmit it with its purity, has the following general effects:

1. It gives you energy on three levels: physical, emotional, and mental.
2. It creates transformation in your nature.
3. It creates detachment but inclusiveness.
4. It develops the sense of Infinity.
5. It develops the sense of freedom and joy.
6. It creates striving and beauty toward perfection.

When you hear music and feel exhausted or mentally diffused, or if you become forgetful and lazy, change the music. Real music nourishes your nervous system and stimulates your etheric centers. Your digestion improves, your memory becomes sharper, you feel that you are awake, your observation is keen, and you enjoy solving problems.

Good music creates equilibrium in your emotional nature, if the past recordings are totally wiped away. Transformation in your nature takes place. You change the way you think, feel, and act. You feel a drive to be noble, honest, and trustworthy. You keep your word. You do not manipulate your friends or any other person.

Detachment slowly appears in your soul. You no longer exercise attachment or "stickiness" to things and people. Material things lose their power over you. Even so-called love and sex do not control you and your way of thinking. But such a detachment does not make you an isolated being. On the contrary, you detach from forms and objects of desire, but you identify with beauty, wisdom, and the spirit found in any person or form.

You become inclusive and tolerant mentally, but nothing can enslave you or manipulate you.

The sense of Infinity is a very rare sense. Through this sense, the person sees Infinity and lives in Infinity — in the world of endlessness. For such a person, all living forms have Infinity in them. He knows that this Infinity will always be with him, so he relates himself to people or to living forms not in terms of short contacts but in terms of infinite duration. This is why on the long path of Infinity he wants to travel with those who love him, with those in whom he created beauty, with those who are free, with those whom he did not hurt or deceive, with those against whom he did not commit crimes. One does not need to travel with those who hate him, with those whom he hated, with those whom he exploited, with those who deceived and committed every kind of crime. The sense of Infinity develops in a person the eternal presence of all that is.

Real music cultivates in you the sense of beauty, joy, and freedom. People are not yet aware that our senses, especially the higher senses, develop through sound.

The sense of beauty is a very subtle sense, and through it man can not only see rare beauty but also enjoy rare beauty.

The sense of joy is a unique sense. It registers the joy of flowers, trees, mountains, and stars. It registers the joy of hearts and the joy found in higher realms. A person with the sense of joy can register transcendental joy from Nature.

The sense of beauty also sees the ugliness behind an artificially fabricated beauty. No artificial beauty can attract a person who has the sense of beauty because in a small expression the complete ugliness reveals itself to him.

The sense of freedom is a very mysterious sense. It keeps a person from being caught in his urges, drives, glamors, and illusions. Immediately he senses such obstacles around him and does not let people enslave him with their own urges, drives, glamors, and illusions. The sense of freedom warns immediately when any danger to his freedom appears.

High-level music develops these unique senses.

Higher music increases in you the power of striving — striving toward improvement, betterment, and perfection. It mobilizes your higher centers in such a way that they slowly increase their pressure upon your personality and create in it various sublimations and changes. Man sometimes feels that something within him is urging him to climb, to go forward and gain victories over his nature, and to direct his soul toward the stars.

Sometimes great achievements are crowned by tears. People think that such tears are tears of joy, but they mean more than that. As a person strives and climbs new heights, greater Infinity reveals itself before his eyes and he feels humiliated by his achievements. He also remembers how much time he wasted in useless persuasions. But through such tears, the striving one dares for new victories, even conquering the memories of his past failures.

Real music reveals to you the image of your distant future and gives you a chance to see the condition you are in, or that you were in.

On the physical level, good music

1. coordinates the organs and glands and improves the circulation
2. gives energy
3. purifies the body of decaying elements
4. heals
5. puts the body in contact with the constructive energies in the Universe

On the emotional level, good music

1. colors the emotions
2. expels the negative ones
3. refines the emotions
4. creates aspiration
5. heals the emotional body of the wounds of hatred, anger, fear, greed, and jealousy
6. coordinates the chakras
7. establishes contact with etheric and mental centers

On the mental level, good music

1. brings serenity and peace
2. strengthens the power of creative imagination and visualization
3. establishes receptivity for higher inspiration and impressions
4. stimulates creativity

5. develops the power to synthesize

6. creates the power of detachment

7. organizes the mental centers and relates them to the centers of the astral and etheric bodies and to the glands of the physical body

People have the misconception that certain music belongs to certain nations. It is true that music can be colored by national characteristics, but good music breaks the boundaries of a particular nation and becomes universal. Music that cannot be universal is not real music. There is only one music — world music, universal music. Beauty is not the property of anyone. Beauty belongs to all nations equally.

Man contacts music consciously when his physical ears register the sound waves and consciously evaluate them. When the mental and etheric-physical ears fuse, unfold, and integrate, man can hear thoughts. Many people converse mentally. It is at this stage that the subtle eye begins to operate and sees the colors of each note and their subtle formation in space. One can enjoy music through his eyes and ears by watching the colors and hearing the notes.

When the physical-etheric and mental ears fuse, unfold, and integrate, man develops the capacity to hear the music of the Subtle Worlds. When the astral and physical-etheric ears fuse, after the fusion of the physical-etheric and mental ears, the person also hears the music of flowers and trees.

In higher psychism, the mental and physical-etheric ears must be developed first. If the astral and physical-etheric ears develop before the mental ears, one falls into lower psychism because he can discriminate neither the sounds nor the origins of the sounds nor their meaning. Discrimination and accuracy come from the mental ears fused with the physical-etheric ears.

When you are ready to listen to good music, first you must have a good machine — a good stereo or tape recorder and good speakers. If the machine is of low quality, it distorts the music. Distorted music can have a bad effect on your etheric, astral, and mental centers as does a vitamin that is rotten or moldy. If you are listening to a recording, it must be in the best condition. If the music is live, the musical instruments must be well-tuned. If the instruments are not in tune, the notes will disturb the centers and create health problems.

Relaxation is very important. People do not listen to music in a relaxed state of body, emotions, and mind. Physical relaxation is the first step because different tensions in your body have different reactions to the music. For example, if you hit a ball against a stone wall, the ball bounces back strongly. But if you hit the ball against a wool curtain, the ball falls in front of the curtain. Tense areas in the body receive a heavier impact of the music, and relaxed areas receive it without reaction.

To create a uniform impact of music upon your body, the body must be totally relaxed; then the music will penetrate every part of it. The purpose of the music in this case is to create harmony within your body. Harmony will bring health, strength, and vitality and will regenerate your whole system.

Only a relaxed body can absorb music and regenerate itself. When the body is in harmony, the person feels happy. He can control his body and its urges and drives only when the body is in harmony. Only a tamed horse obeys you. It is in relaxation that you can listen to music with your whole body, spreading your consciousness over your whole body. The consciousness thus acts as an agent of reception of the music throughout your body.

The next step is to be emotionally very quiet. Different types of emotions in you create different reactions to music, as different waves reflect the light of the moon differently. The ocean of your emotions must be calmed as much as possible with a feeling of joy. When an agitated emotional body listens to music, it creates over stimulation in certain parts and depletion in other parts, and the person falls into a deeper state of imbalance.

One can notice how people take extreme actions, attitudes, or decisions after listening to music in an emotionally tensed condition. Sometimes it is our sorrow or suffering that listens to music. Sometimes it is our hatred, jealousy, or revenge that listens to music, and they thus become stronger in our nature.

We have in our emotional body the correspondences of gas formations, smog formations, dust formations, cloud formations, and even force formations, all formed by negative emotions. Each of these formations translates the music through its own interest, and the goal of the music cannot be achieved. The goal of music is, first, to create harmony and rhythm.

Every kind of emotion is a whirlpool of vibrations, and each whirlpool reacts differently to music. Some of them are coils of pain; some of them grief, despair, joy, and so on. When one relaxes and calms his emotions, he pulls his consciousness out of the emotional body and lets the emotions calm down, as a lake does after a storm passes. After listening to the music, the negative whirlpools will lose their intensity and begin to fuse with the whole body of the emotions. Some of them will actually disappear.

If you are not physically and emotionally relaxed while listening to music, certain areas of your body will express signs of discomfort, weakness, or even pain.

Bad music should not, of course, be listened to after such preparations. People listen to bad music when they are in physical and emotional tension, are hateful, full of worries, sexually stimulated, or drunk. In such cases, the bad music disturbs their higher senses and makes them irresponsible persons, indifferent to their duties and responsibilities and to the needs of other people.

The next step is mental serenity, which is the absence of anxiety, worry, fear, superstitions, illusions, and vanity. Let all such tensions depart from your mind and disappear. If you listen to music with mental tension and such mental formations, you will create disturbances in your mental aura because your anxieties, fears, and worries will absorb the energy of the music and become stronger and more violent.

One must thus listen to music with his whole body, with all his organs, as if his body were a huge ear. He must listen to music simultaneously with his emotional and mental bodies. Then he will experience that through his triple nature the music flows — healing, purifying, strengthening, and harmonizing all the centers, glands, and organs — and that the whole personality enters a state of transformation.

You can even listen to music with your nails, eyelashes, and teeth. When you listen to music according to these suggestions, observe for a few seconds how different parts of your body are registering the music. Especially watch people who listen to music in the ways described.

Music therapy is one of the sciences of the future, but it needs sophisticated apparatuses or clairvoyance and clairaudience or vast experience to apply it for healing and for transformation. Some clairvoyants tell us about the unfoldments and color formations going on in the etheric centers during a piece of music: how a network of rays is forming between the centers of various bodies; how the heart center is expanding and connecting itself with the Chalice and absorbing prana from space. The time of listening to music is a time of Holy Communion with the Higher Worlds.

The eye is also very sensitive to music, especially the pupil and the iris. It would not be an exaggeration to say that good music heals the eyes and bad music causes strain to the eyes. Bad music is responsible for most eye troubles.

One must closely observe the eyes and changes in vision after listening to music. This can be done with children in schools, thus finding the best music to play for them.

Watch yourself and others listening to music while driving a car. Watch the physical body, the emotional expressions, and the mental behavior. You can watch yourself and ask others to report their experiences. If the music does not make you alert mentally, calm emotionally, and relaxed physically, you will find yourself in danger and perhaps you will awaken in a hospital.

In listening to music you submit yourself to chemical changes. Past chemical formations and present chemical formations may agree or disagree. It is you who will intelligently control the chemistry of your body, emotions, and mind. Certain combinations are destructive and explosive. Certain combinations are healthy and beneficial. Through observation you will eventually learn to produce a better chemistry in your system. This is very important because it is through the chemistry of your body that you can control the planetary, solar, and zodiacal influences.

During the full moon, when you know what kind of energy is more influential in the sphere of the earth, you will create the chemistry in your nature that is harmonious with the incoming energies. This chemistry can be created with the proper high-level music that not only produces the needed elements in you but also helps to create a new chemistry between you and the Rays of the ruling signs.

Steps for Listening to Music

1. Physical relaxation
2. Emotional quietness
3. Mental serenity
4. Elimination of worries and anxieties
5. Concentration on the music, following its moves and listening with your entire body
6. Visualizing that the music is purifying your etheric, astral, and mental bodies
7. Visualizing how it is coordinating, healing, and tuning all your vehicles
8. Visualizing how you are building communication lines with Higher Beings

Listening must not be longer than ten minutes. At the beginning, even six minutes is too much. When the music ends, sit quietly until your aura settles down.

After six months of experience with music, you can do the following:

1. Continue to listen to music in a relaxed state.
2. Dance or do movements to it.

3. Read, write, or paint with music.

4. Talk or give a lecture while music is playing.

5. Eat with music.

6. Embrace someone while listening to music.

7. Pray or meditate with music.

It is recommended that you do not play music while you sleep. It may stimulate your brain and create associative disturbances. It may also keep you on lower planes and not let you engage in your higher responsibilities.

In the future, a kind of music will be composed that can be used to assist your withdrawal from the body and to raise yourself into higher spheres. Such music will be composed by those who are knowledgeable about astral, mental, and spatial music.

The location where you listen to music is very important. It must fit the music and also your goal in listening to the music. The location must be restful, comfortable, beautiful, and quiet. You can also light candles. You can listen to music near the sound of waterfalls, rivers, oceans, or wind in the trees. Play the music softly.

Ways of listening

It is important that people not only listen to music but also use music as a means of unfoldment and as an expression of consciousness. There are many ways to listen to music:

1. One must learn how to hear the music in a color, visualizing notes as a sequence of colors, colors that are not usual.

2. One can visualize these colors in various geometrical or natural forms of flowers, then petals and colors.

3. One can visualize geometrical forms in harmonious movement with each other.

4. One can visualize fragrance emanating from every note.

5. One can visualize a beautiful dance in harmony with the music.

6. One can visualize a process of purification, healing, and sublimation of all vehicles, through music and of contacting the Inner Core.

7. One can visualize some mysterious ceremonies and rituals for spiritual attainment.

8. One can visualize in intense concentration a transformation process through music.

9. One can visualize through music a beautiful change in others and transformation of their nature.

In doing such visualizations you will discover more advanced uses of the music that will enable you to create, to purify, to heal, and to contact higher sources of guidance and inspiration not only for yourself, but also for those whom you love or for those whom you aspire to transform.

What music does

1. Music has the power to dispel old elements and forms. Combined with thought and visualization, it can be a potent way for creative work. You must choose music that fits your visualization, not music that agitates your emotions and disturbs your visualization.

2. Music also helps you attract purer elements into your nature, destroy the old thoughtforms, and stimulate latent seeds of beauty.

3. Music creates communication with your Solar Angel and with those beings who watch your evolution. Music is so important that dark forces do all that is possible to make people use it as a means for degeneration. It is very important to learn how to listen to music in deep concentration and involvement.

4 Music can also help you detach yourself from your bodies and pass on to higher planes of existence. There is special music that helps you withdraw when your vehicles are prepared to let you go.

All universal creativity is carried out by music — inaudible to our average ears.

All forms are embodiments of music. Beauty of form is the result of harmony of sound.

Musical Instruments

1. Wind instruments affect the emotions.
2. Brass instruments affect the etheric body and the emotions.
3. Strings are *kama-manasic* in nature; they affect the higher emotions and lower mind.
4. Piano music affects the abstract mind, the atmic level, and also the lower or concrete mind.
5. Drums affect the etheric centers.
6. The santur affects the emotions and the Intuition.
7. The harp affects the subconsciousness and the Chalice.
8. The voice can act on all levels, according to the level of the singer or the listener.

It is also possible to impose on various instruments your own level, or to misuse them for different ends.

After a long experience in good listening, you can experiment with various things, for example:

1. You can concentrate on flowers and trees and energize them.
2. You can concentrate your mind on your friends to comfort them, to heal them, to uplift them. You are transmitting not the music but your elevated thoughts for healing, comfort, and beauty. Music has the power to amplify your best thoughts.

3. You can think of a certain animal or of animals as a whole and send them your love and compassion.

4. You can send thoughts of peace and understanding to space.

5. You can send thoughts of peace to certain conventions and meetings while listening to music.

6. You can build your continuity of consciousness and attempt to contact your Soul, higher planes, even your Master while listening to music.

The main rule is that you will try always to be in your tower of calmness, peace, and serenity to be effective. Involvement with problems, emotionally and mentally, destroys the effectiveness of your work. This is why these things must not be attempted until you really know how to listen to music.

One falls into glamors if he is focused in astral consciousness.

A man who has reached perfection in three levels and is fused with his Soul is a unique manifestation of music. This is a factual statement and not a mystical dream. All the organs, glands, centers, and systems eventually develop their proper frequencies and integrate and align. They first produce various melodies. Then the symphony emerges. Thus a man becomes a living music in Nature.

Of course, the evolution of man does not stop there. As he advances, he becomes a part of solar music, zodiacal music, galactic music.

If once our ear opens in higher states of consciousness, we will see that the whole Creation is music that is based on three concepts — harmony, unity, and synthesis — and that to act against these principles creates disturbances with painful consequences.

Music is called the language of the gods. It is so beautiful to remember a statement made centuries ago — "God sang, and as He was singing the Archetypes of all manifestation began to appear in space."

Manifestation is densified music.

Chapter 6

Rhythm and Centers

Every great musician and every Temple musician knows the value of rhythm. It is a great science based primarily on clairvoyant or intuitive investigations.

Rhythm is related to the centers, or chakras. Each center has its own special *pulsation* — its rhythm. Rhythm can be utilized for various purposes:

1. It kindles the dormant centers.
2. It purifies the blocked centers.
3. It balances overactive centers.
4. It creates harmony between all centers.
5. It arouses the fire of a special center in order to use the energy for a certain purpose or for the expansion of consciousness. It is known that

the centers have special influences on the body, emotions, and mind and on our consciousness.

6. It establishes links with angelic kingdoms which inspire us with lofty aspirations and inspiration.

7. It establishes links with the earth-Soul in order to come to our common sense and normalize ourselves.

The science of rhythm was available many thousands of years ago. It was used to regulate sexual drives, to heal the sick, to inspire people to be fearless and joyfully enter into war. In addition, rhythm was used to peacefully pass away, to contact Angels and to receive guidance from Them. But gradually the science was withdrawn as people began to use it for pleasures and to hurt people and captivate them for self-interest.

Some of the music of today is the degenerated remains of the past.

Rhythm is the reflection of the beat of the centers. Fundamentally there are seven major beats corresponding to the seven major centers. There is a rhythmic beat which arouses the fire of kundalini, another one for the sacral center, another one for the solar plexus, and others for the heart, throat, ajna, and head centers.

There are also subtle rhythms mixed with the basic rhythms of the seven etheric chakras. These subtle rhythms affect seven astral centers and create seven basic moods:

- joy
- excitement
- enthusiasm
- fear
- anger
- depression
- revenge

There are still more subtle rhythms mixed with these rhythms that are related to the mental centers. This is the fourth kind of rhythm.

The fifth kind of rhythm is called human rhythm, which awakens the human soul.

The sixth one is called the rhythm of the Chalice, which influences the twelve-petaled Chalice in the higher mind and makes it available so that the human soul can have contact with the Treasury of the Chalice.

The seventh rhythm is called the fiery rhythm. It is related to the Inner Presence in man, which some esotericists call the Solar Angel or the Transpersonal Self. Gradually this science will be given to the musicians and scientists when enough confidence is established for their right use.

Scientists will use the energy of sound more and more. But they will not be able to make real use of sound until they know the science of rhythm.

There are many secrets in the *Vedas* about sound and rhythm.

Rhythmic sound in the future can do most of the jobs that electricity is doing now.

People do not realize that they are exposed daily to various rhythms: the rhythm of trains, cars, bicycles, horses, mules, donkeys; various rhythms of Nature such as waterfalls, rivers, waves of oceans, the roosters; mechanical rhythms such as refrigerators and other electrical devices. We are subjected to various rhythms that create various and ever changing moods within us.

If you are sitting in your car and you see cars passing in a different rhythm; if you listen to a lecture delivered in a different rhythm; if you are in a train and you are subject to different rhythms of the railways; if you are living close to an airport and you are subject to the flights and their noise; if you are listening to the birds in the morning and at dusk; if you are bombarded by various rhythms of electrical objects; if you are in the ocean or in a waterfall and exposed to different rhythms — know that every individual rhythm contributes to your health, happiness, prosperity, and moods or it deprives you of your enthusiasm and joy and makes you irritable and full of anger or apathy.

Big construction machinery, the rhythm of construction workers, the various rhythms of music we hear every day around us from our television and radio sets, from our tapes, etc., all these rhythms affect us unconsciously, and we go from one mood to another constantly without knowing why.

The dangerous thing is that some moods bring our consciousness so low that we do obnoxious things and then regret it. Many negative thoughts, negative emotions, and destructive actions are taken during such moods, and often these are the moments that destroy our life. Especially when rhythms are associated with hypnotic suggestions, they become very dangerous. People do not realize that their life, in a very high percentage, is controlled by the rhythm of the moment.

When people discover the secrets of the pulsations of the centers, they will compose rhythmic sequences to operate on those centers for various reasons. For example, a certain rhythm is very beneficial during childbirth. The recovery of a mother needs another rhythm. The growing child needs another rhythm until he is fourteen months old. Sexual relations need a three dimensional rhythm, if the purpose is to conceive an advanced child.

Opportunists will be ready to create certain musical rhythms to collect money, claiming that their music can do such and such a job. Hence again we can enter into the domain of exploitation.

There are only a few musicians at the present time who are able to see, clairvoyantly, the pulsation of the chakras and observe the influence of various rhythms on them. There are those people who are advanced enough to come in contact with subtle rhythms and translate them in their compositions.

The creativity of some artists increases in listening to certain music that has the proper rhythm.

Others lose their creativity, their logic and reasoning, even their good heart by exposing themselves to certain destructive rhythms.

As our consciousness expands our pulsation changes, as well as the rhythm that is beneficial for us. Some people heal themselves by dancing. Others permanently hurt themselves in the same rhythm. People can develop sensitivity to rhythm and ascertain if the rhythm is good for them for dancing or even for listening.

Many people's consciousness petrifies and their spiritual visions are lost when they expose themselves to certain music. They change sometimes one hundred eighty degrees without noticing how their consciousness, judgment, and values have entered a path of degeneration.

Certain societies know the power of rhythm, and the leaders forbid certain music to enter their country.

Some leaders control their population with music that destroys in them the urge for freedom, their courage and daring. Eventually they create sheep instead of human beings of dignity.

On the other hand we have the music of great spiritual leaders, such as the real Sufis, Buddhists, Druses, Christians, and mystics. Some churches still use the original music of the Roman Catholic Church, the Armenian Church music, and Russian Orthodox Church

music. The spiritual rhythm in their chanting and singing opens the higher chakras.

But very little of their music remains as it was
originally. Modern vanity introduced its changes, and
even to a degree they have reverted to dangerous instruments. But, still, the original music is available in the
Far East in some Buddhist and Christian Monasteries,
and even in some Jewish Temples and Mohammedan
Mosques.

Protection against undesirable rhythms can be
achieved only by psychic energy or by living in subter-
ranean caves. Psychic energy builds a shield around
you that operates either as a shock absorber or as a
reflector.

This is why in the early morning every day one
must put his personality under the rhythm of the Divine
Presence in him through prayers and meditation. After
charging yourself with the rhythm of the Soul you can
create enough protection from all the daily, many colored rhythms that do not work in your favor.

Daily we must express our gratitude:

1. To the Almighty Presence in everything, everywhere

2. To His Creation for the Beauty in which we
   live

3. To the Hierarchy for its protection and guidance

4. To the Eternal Youth for His sacrifice

5. For all our Teachers who illuminated our path and challenged us to bloom

6. To our parents who brought us to this earth

7. To our wife, husband, children, to our friends and co-workers

And close with OM OM OM

We know about the rhythm of the seasons, the rhythm of day and night, the rhythm of the moon and zodiacal contacts, but there is also in space the rhythm of explosions that, like the beat of a drum, affects our systems in different cycles and in different ways. In the future, it will be possible to cooperate with the rhythm of explosions.

There are also rhythms of far off stars that emit most powerful rays in space and rhythmically touch our planet.

What a great illumination will come to mankind when such rhythms are offered to us through research, observation, or direct revelation.

The rhythm of Nature is always regenerating. We have experiences about the rhythm of ocean waves, the rhythm of waterfalls, winds, the motion of the trees, the rhythmic pulsation of the Mother Earth itself. Our hearts are recorders of all rhythms.

Chapter 7

Rhythm and Matter

Rhythm comes into being when the spirit or energy tries to manifest regularly through matter. The measured resistance and response of the matter creates rhythm.

When spirit acts, matter reacts for a given time until it enables itself to respond. These regular responses create rhythm. Thus, through rhythm the spirit manifests.

There are many hundreds of kinds of rhythm, according to the composition of matter. Some matter of a plane needs time to respond to the spirit: some in this or that interval.

The change of rhythm is the change of the response of matter.

Man creates rhythm according to his level and the substance in which his consciousness is anchored.

He has a rhythm of responding or reacting to the impulse of his Soul, or the impulse of his spirit. His responses have various patterns or rhythms that he uses to spread the influence of the spirit.

The more he enters into rhythm, the more he becomes healthy, happy, successful, and conscious.

One of man's expression is music. Music can be rhythmic or not. Rhythmic music has a mantric effect upon the surroundings. It quickens, kindles the fires in the bodies, and eases the transmission of the spirit. If a drum accompanies the music, the pulsation of the matter manifests under the rhythm of the centers of the etheric body.

We must realize that the central power of the Universe, which is called the Cosmic Magnet, has Its own rhythm and Its rhythm is different on each Cosmic Plane of substance. Actually, all forms on these planes are the result of the rhythm of the Cosmic Magnet. Thus, esotericism suggests that there are 336 kinds of rhythm. There are 49 major rhythms and 287 minor rhythms in the Universe. Living forms try to adjust themselves to such rhythms.

Pulsations of atoms and cells on any level are rhythmic in expression. They are formed by the rhythm of exchange of time between matter and spirit, consciousness and matter, Soul and personality, a leader and a group.

Synchronization of rhythms is the path of cooperation. Simultaneity of rhythm is an achievement.

Rhythm has many qualities:

• There are sounds in rhythm.

• There are colors in rhythm.

• There are movements in rhythm.

• There are feelings in rhythm.

• There are actions in rhythm.

Synchronization of all these rhythms leads to integration with personality, alignment with the Soul, and harmonization with the Cosmic Magnet.

Chapter 8

Mystery of Rhythm

Rhythm is built by pause and beat. The measure in pause and beat may change, for example:

123•123•123•

This is a rhythm that is based on

♩ = ♪   ♪ = ♪

1 = ♪

2 = ♪

3 = ♪

Another rhythm can be

Rhythm is a combination of measures and pauses. There are usual rhythms, and there are unusual rhythms that seem very complicated, for example:

All of Nature is in rhythm. Our earth has its rhythm, the solar system has its own rhythm, the galaxy has its own rhythm, and every human being has his own rhythm. His rhythm is his heartbeat, the pulsations of his centers, and the rhythm of the circulation of fire through the centers.

Rhythm is not in sound only. It is in the arrangements of color as well. The most magnetic arrangements have a specific color in them.

Rhythm is also in motion and in speech. There is chaotic motion and rhythmic motion, as there is in speech.

Speech and motion can form a group rhythm that can cancel out each other or support each other. Rhythm leads to order, cooperation, and beauty — to Cosmos.

Rhythm in a group is the coordination of the individual rhythms. Fifty drums can be coordinated in such a way that each one's rhythm supports and compliments the rhythm of the others.

The best leaders are conductors of rhythms. The conductor can organize a group rhythm if each member is in rhythmic meditation, study, and service.

We must remember that an expansion of consciousness changes the rhythm of the person.

If we want to have a group, we must see to it that the changing rhythms of the members are in harmony with each other. Such adjustments of rhythm occur naturally if everyone strives to improve his life and abstain from

- slander
- criticism
- self-imposition
- vanity
- ego

and instead use

- understanding
- love
- cooperation

and remember the purpose that brought them together.

As a healthy body adjusts itself with the rhythm of the heart, so every individual adjusts his or her rhythm to the dominating rhythm of the group purpose.

There are rhythms that involve one second, hours, days, lives, even hundreds or thousands or millions of years. We often call these "cycles." A cycle is the end or the beginning of a rhythm that is related to events instead of to sound — events such as wars, earthquakes, typhoons, tornadoes, comets, epidemics, and the weather.

It is interesting to know that as a human being integrates the rhythms of all the vehicles of his nature, so does Nature or a Planetary, Solar, or Galactic Soul. And it is possible that some of these Souls create disturbances within Their rhythms.

Any time the rhythm is broken, the cycle changes; and when rhythm and cycle are distorted, destructive events happen in the vehicles of these Souls.

These destructive events are the efforts to reestablish the rhythm, annihilating the causes and effects of those actions which brought disturbances in the rhythm.

Every disturbance on any level, in any form, is the result of a disturbance of rhythm.

Human beings try to change or cause changes in the natural rhythm by introducing actions and elements that speed or retard the rhythm and cycles, and this creates a chain of reactions here on earth and in the Higher Worlds.

Death and incarnation are in the rhythm. Nature forces all that are out of rhythm to enter into rhythm.

Our whole galaxy runs on its complicated rhythm system.

One day our computers will be used to explain the symphony of various rhythms and how they fit and co-operate with each other to keep the music going on in a Cosmic scale and to actualize the purpose of the Great Life Whose body is our galaxy.

Every single atom or cell or form is pulled into the whirlpool of that galactic rhythm.

All music, all songs and sound produced on the earth either help the overall rhythm or distort it.

For example, we are told that explosions destroy the rhythm of the flow of energies in Nature. We are even told that we must not fire a single gun, as it is very disastrous at this time to the equilibrium of the planet. Equilibrium is the balance of various rhythms.

We contact the real rhythm of Nature — which is the body of the Planetary Logos — by raising our awareness to our mental plane.

Our mental plane is the physical body of the Planetary Logos, and our higher mental plane corresponds to His etheric body. In the higher mental plane our rhythm synchronizes with the rhythm of His energy body.

Let us examine the following diagrams:

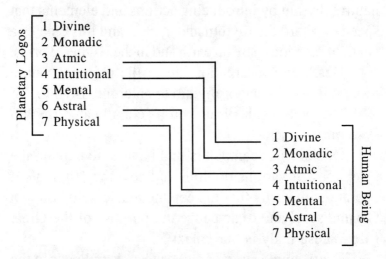

As our consciousness goes to higher planes, we synchronize with the deeper layers of rhythm and cycles of the Planetary Logos, and in the meantime we synchronize with the rhythms of the Solar Consciousness.

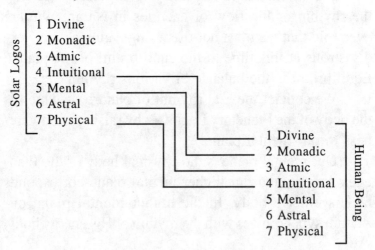

Try to understand these charts and try to realize the complexity of the rhythm into which you are entering. Progress is impossible if you do not synchronize your rhythm with the rhythm of the higher Life in which you live and move and have your being.

Your rhythm must tune in — so to say — with a higher rhythm and find a right place in the symphony of the higher rhythm.

Our progress is to be a part of the rhythm in the planetary Chalice, and then graduate into the rhythm of the Chalice of the Solar Logos.

All of existence pulsates with rhythm directed by the heartbeat of the Cosmic Heart.

There is a time of receiving and a time of giving. Rhythm is the basic system of this process. Beat gives; pause receives. Every different beat evokes a different flow of energy and passes on a different flow of energy. A beat on a higher plane may correspond to a beat on a lower plane, but has a tremendously higher potency of creativity than the beat of the lower plane.

Creativity is the result of an organized, rhythmic process. There are times of inspiration; there are times of expression. If they are not rhythmic, there is disturbance between the ebb and flow, between reception and expression.

In the greatest art, the beat and pause are regulated in the most creative potentiality that is progressively acted out on higher levels.

Some arts project multidimensional rhythm and become the most powerful instruments of transformation.

Have a time daily to synchronize yourself with the higher rhythm existing within you and within the planetary and solar auras.

A few minutes daily will bring miraculous changes in your life and creative abilities.[1]

1. See, for example: *Daily Discipline of Worship* and *Daily Spiritual Striving*.

Chapter 9

Four Types of Music

The creativity of music is divided into four types.

1. The first type of music is created by our blind physical urges and drives, by our glamors, illusions, by hypnotic suggestions, hate, anger, fear, jealousy, revenge, or by our vanity. This is the music that for centuries has kept humanity in captivity. It is mechanical, without vision, meaning, and inner purpose.

2. The second type of music is the result of sexual heat, or the result of overwhelming emotion, pain, love, pleasure, or of many subtle feelings and emotions related to many emotional and mental states.This type of music is a spontaneous outpouring of stimulated human glands, centers, and ganglia.

In certain countries when, for example, a woman is in sorrow or grief or in ecstasy, she sings or plays her own music to express her pain or joy. Then others add words to such songs and they become popular music.

The same is true for religious aspirations that effortlessly create song or music. I have known many people in the old country who, to mourn their beloved ones, created music and words and song.

3. The third type of music is created by those people who are not their emotions or thoughts and can act independently of the interference of their urges, glamors, and illusions, but they serve the will to dominate their egos. It is this type of music that is increasing now and spreading everywhere, slowly becoming an instrument to control the lives of individuals, groups, and nations. This music has a very powerful subliminal element that in the future may be used for totalitarian power anywhere.

4. The fourth type of music is created by those who feel the need to help the Creative Sound carry out its purpose of freedom and resurrection. This music is created not by personalities, not by egos, but by those who have access to the Plan and Purpose of life, and they compose their music

      a. To release the prisoners of bodies, emotions, and thoughts and help them be their True Self

      b. To spread Beauty, Goodness, Righteousness, Joy, and Freedom

    c. To help people bloom in their innate beauty

    d. To develop group consciousness in people

    e. To put people in contact with the greater centers of wisdom and power on this planet and in the solar system

This music has a very complicated geometry and arithmetic, and its rhythm is arranged in such a way that it stimulates the fires in man to circulate properly and fuse gradually on higher and higher planes.

At present, these four kinds of music present

1. The prostituted use of sound

2. The spontaneous creative music

3. The manipulated use of sound

4. The conscious and benevolent use of sound by those who have inner spiritual achievements

The future of culture and civilization will depend on these four kinds of music. If the first type of music predominates, we will have a world that we have known for some five thousand years: wars, bloodshed, genocide, destruction, hatred, revenge, obsession, possession, insanity, and diseases.

If the second type of music predominates, we will toss in the sea of emotions, in pain and in pleasure. If the third type of music predominates, we will have certain groups of people or strong and wealthy individuals dominating multitudes, using them for their pleasure and plans. This will reach a degree in which anyone eventually will be able to control the

- health
- mood
- mind
- will

of people. The real age of slavery will come and, with it, massive destruction and calamities.

If the fourth type of music predominates, we will see the door of a new life. People will strive to reach their inner divinity and release its potentials and beauty. The culture of humanity will reach levels never imagined before.

Science will penetrate into Cosmic spheres. Human relationships will shine with the substance of compassion. Each human relationship will characterize itself as a symphony.

Man will use the Intuition, freedom, and joy, and the misery of the world will slowly melt away like an iceberg in the ocean of joy and bliss. Through music it will be possible to annihilate all diseases, and man will be born through music, live in music, and pass away through music. The cause of death will be mainly the intention to live on higher spheres than the physical plane. The new music will slowly annihilate the walls existing between higher planes of existence, and people will consciously prepare themselves to live in one of those planes, rather than on the physical plane, to carry on their spiritual evolution. The spiritual evolution will be understood as the blooming and flowering of all inner potentials that Nature put within the Core of man. Of course, the music will create ceremonies, with colors and movements and rituals that will assist self-actualization for people.

Those who will live in such an age will testify about the past ignorance of humanity and be witnesses of this self-destructive music.

In the future, music will be created along each Ray of the Seven Rays. It will be used

    a. To release these Rays into activity

    b. To direct them to constructive channels

    c. To change the focus of the soul from one Ray to another

    d. To change the Rays of the personality vehicles, Soul, etc.

    e. To help people substantiate their own Rays according to their need

    f. To learn how to contact the Sources of their Rays, thus accumulating wisdom, compassion, and power

    g. To contact the higher mind through the instrumentality of the Rays

The music of the future will be used also to clean pollution on physical, emotional, and mental spheres and to let the Divine Ray of Creativity pass to the globe with all Its purity and wealth.

Of course, manipulative and destructive music will continue to fight for its own interests, but certain people will begin to see the results of such music and encourage the population to listen to the new music. They will convince their children to stay away from such music. In the beginning music will be discriminated only by the heart, and later by observing the affects.

Manipulative music will be more difficult to cast away because it will penetrate, through its subliminal power, to the mechanisms of people's consciousness and for a long time will not let them see the light of a new day. Of course science will eventually find ways and means to detect subliminal messages. But such music will do its damage to millions of people on earth for a long time.

These four kinds of music not only affect the living people but also those who have departed and live in various spheres of existence. There are no borders for music. Each kind of music penetrates into Cosmos, into all existence. We will not be surprised in the future when, from Venus, they will tell us that our music is bothering them!

The future of humanity must be built by the fourth kind of music, based on Intuition, and elevated by lofty inspirations and on impressions coming from Higher Worlds.

Chapter 10

Music in the Future

It is hoped that in the near future, within one hundred years, the Adepts of music will come into incarnation to use sound and music as a service for humanity, to alleviate physical, emotional, and mental pain and suffering, and to start the age of Aquarius.

This music will be the combination of science, inspiration, and impression.

The composers, according to the need of the individual group and nation, will prepare specific pieces to meet the specific need.

In the future it will not be a surprise if your physician prescribes a piece of music to heal your indigestion or wipe out your headache.

The quality of each note and the combination with other notes will be the supreme science. This will be called musical chemistry and frequency, and it will be offered to the body directly or to the ears indirectly.

Sound created the whole Universe. The combinations of sound are responsible for all the diversity in the Universe.

Sound creates; sound destroys. Sound brings into revelation; sound annihilates all that exists. Every virus, microbe, germ is a sound, and sound can annihilate them as particular and harmful sounds.

The Magi of sound and music will be Those Who will have electronics, chemistry, musical, and inspirational backgrounds. They will be scientists. They will be able to receive inspiration from higher sources of music, and also They will have enough preparation to receive impressions of supreme ideas which will be put into musical forms.

It will be possible through sound to move mountains and huge rocks and build castles of beauty through music.

Music will be used to create harmony and cooperation and peace in the world.

The purpose of the music of the future is to do the following:

1. Invigorate the cells and atoms in the vehicles of man

2. Create integration and health

3. Stimulate the glands and chakras through expanding the consciousness

4. Eradicate disorders and attacks to the body, emotions, and mental nature

5. Protect the vehicles of man from attacks of germs and hostile viruses in Nature

6. Provide "sunshine and food" for the chakras to bloom in harmonious ways

7. Stimulate sensitivity in the emotions and clarity and sharpness in the mind

8. Increase striving and labor for perfection

9. Encourage heroic acts, fearlessness, and daring

10. Create a breakthrough between the visible and the Subtle Worlds

11. Enable man to have contact with his heart and conscience and to reveal the sense of responsibility

12. Cause the blooming of his Chalice

13. Realize the brotherhood of humanity

14. Realize one's own divinity

15. Develop forgiveness, gratitude, and bliss

To actualize such a vision, a new breed of composers will soon appear in the world, and the science of sound, with all its mysteries, will be available to them.

We are told that future geniuses will create such musical compositions that in comparison with them, the present masterpieces of music will be considered children's songs.

Future laboratories of music will be built on several acres just to accommodate the scientific machines and instruments of music. There, the most qualified computer-scientists will work and analyze every piece of music by any composer. They will properly evaluate its relation to its purpose, and recommend its use only if it justifies the purpose for which it was created. The human brain is the outer formation of a sound of a note, or notes, released continuously by the human soul and Solar Angel.

The quality and usefulness of a person is the mixture of the initial notes plus the music to which he is exposed during his life.

We seldom realize that the colors of Nature and the environment are music. The forms are music. The music of a forest is different from the music of a river or ocean. The music of rocks is different from the music of sand. The music of a sphere is different from the square, triangle, or cube.

Scientific information will come to us in the future, in relation to where to live in order to bring the best out of us.

Music specifically will be used to grow vegetables, flowers, and shrubs. The future use of music will be scientifically accurate and *controlled.*

There is a tendency to play with Nature, injecting certain substances into trees and shrubs. People may think this is an example of control but the true control of the future will be used not on the objects of experiment but over the method of the experiment itself. The purpose of the control is not to damage the natural order of the vegetable kingdom but to help them reveal their beauty by providing all that is needed by them.

It is possible to cooperate with the lower kingdoms without interfering with their natural tendencies. Music in the future will create such an atmosphere in the vegetable kingdom that their potentials will find ways to manifest themselves.

People might think that this is outrageous to say that music will be used also to help the climate readjust itself and to engage in its natural order. Nature knows what to do and what is best for its creatures.

Whenever man discovers certain laws he tries to force his will on Nature and tries to change it with drastic consequences. Future scientists, knowing what damage we did to Nature, will prefer to cooperate instead of forcing their shortsighted will upon Nature.

Man can help Nature to recover, but he must not attempt to change its course.

We have already induced enough damage to forests, oceans, space, rivers through our wars, poisonous gasses, radioactivity, and toxins. It is a miracle that such an abused Mother still provides nourishment and comfort to Her children.

In the future it will be possible to heal and restore Nature and slowly eliminate causes that deeply damaged it by using scientifically and inspirationally created music.

Humanity is advancing with giant steps in the science of computers and multicolored space sciences. But the main key in the sciences will be not to exploit and manipulate Nature and bring it under the shortsighted interests of human beings but to cooperate with it. The key of the New Era will be cooperation with Nature leading to Synthesis. This task will be in the hands of the musicians.

✧

Chapter 11

Tool of Transformation

A further breakthrough in music is related to the audience. Such an audience will hear this music beyond the range of normal hearing.

Special mirrors will be given to the audience in which they will see the dance of splendid colors the music will create, and they will smell the fragrance of the keys of the notes.

The sound, the color, and the fragrance of the music will uplift and expand the consciousness of the audience.

Such performances of music will help the audience build their collective Antahkarana and come in contact with the presence of the great angelic hosts and Masters.

Such music will also build a strong shield around the planet. The Cosmic evil will find it very hard to reach humanity, and the evil that exists in humanity will gradually vanish.

In the future, music will be created to dissolve hindrances existing in the nature of the individual human being and also hindrances existing among people. These hindrances are etheric, astral, and mental crystallizations that prevent people from communicating with each other. Once such hindrances are removed, right human relations will be rapidly established in humanity. Those who react against such music, because of their fanaticism and separatism, will have a very hard time living on this planet.

This kind of music will also be used to help the vegetable kingdom produce the best trees, flowers, and fruit, and it will help the animal kingdom, especially the birds, to come into a closer relationship with human beings.

Such music will be used not only for healing but also for labor in big factories and offices to raise the productivity and the quality.

For many ages, starting from the year 2025, the keynote of the music will be synthesis and the revelation of the music existing in the higher planes and in Supermundane Ashrams. Such music will create synthesis in all domains of life, and slowly it will cause the sense of synthesis to awaken in advancing human beings.

Through this music people will find the relationship existing in all living forms. The establishment of real communication will be the path leading to ultimate synthesis.

Of course, in coming ages the sense of synthesis will be used as the key to solving all human, planetary, and solar problems.

This music will be used also to facilitate the birth of the human soul in higher mental planes.

There will be a kind of music which may be called *harmonizing and eliminating music.* It will eliminate the devastating effects created by the nerve-shattering noise of mechanical devices, transportation, and explosions and cause them to consume each other or to be harmonized with other creative sounds.

The effects of noise are disastrous for the human future. Certain musicians will be able to destroy the tides of noise before the tides produce destruction, or they will change the rhythm and mix it with constructive sounds to make them creative instead of destructive.

The music in the future will be the foundation of human progress in all fields of human endeavor. It will also be used as medicine for all kinds of diseases and ailments of humanity, instead of injections, pills, or surgery. The use of music will make all our pharmaceuticals obsolete.

We must remember that the origin of everything is sound, and everything will end in sound.

Master musicians will gradually be born in the next century. In comparison with their music, the music of today will be seen as the drumming of the aborigines.

Music will be used to clear the veils existing between etheric, astral, and mental planes, and it will allow human beings to experience the life in such dimensions in their waking consciousness.

The Great Teacher teaches that all existence is a combination of musical notes. Each plane, each dimension has its own note and sub-tones. These forty-nine planes of Creation are seven octaves, the various combinations of which are the Existence. The Creator is a Composer.

In His composition there are two main notes. One is the note of the Spark or Spirit and the other is the note of matter.

In *Cosmic Fire*, the Great Teacher talks about these two notes as follows:

"a. The period of the domination of the form note is that of involution.

"b. The period of the repulsion of form by Spirit [the note] is that of the battlefield of the three worlds [physical, emotional, mental].

"c. The period of attraction of Spirit and Spirit and the consequent withdrawal from form is that of the Path.

"d. The period of domination of the note of Spirit is that of the higher planes of evolution."[1]

He says also, "When spirit and matter sound the same note evolution will cease."[2]

These are very advanced hints for composers and for scientists, and they are very professional formulas which can be used in the music of the future when composers have clear ideas about "the Purpose which the Masters know and serve."[3]

All energies are spiritual notes. All forces are material notes. One must find out how the same note can be spiritual or material. One can find such a difference by studying the science of motives or intentions and the science of psychic energy, together with the events occurring on this Earth.

Future scientists will find out that the nature of the genes in man is arranged by the sound which for ages conditioned them. Once the composer discovers the combination of sounds that will be able to penetrate into the centers of the head which control the genes, then long life on earth will be possible.

The future of humanity can be very bright if greed and separatism do not destroy the planet.

1. *A Treatise on Cosmic Fire* by Alice A. Bailey, p. 275.
2. *Ibid.*
3. From "The Great Invocation."

Chapter 12

Composers

Composers respond to many sources of inspiration or stimulation:

1. Sometimes it is their ego and vanity that compose the music.
2. Sometimes it is the child in them who wanders aimlessly in the fields of sound.
3. Sometimes it is the painful or joyful events in life that inspire them.
4. Sometimes their music is the mechanical performance of their continually changing moods.
5. Sometimes it is the reflection of their feelings about life events.
6. Sometimes the music is an expression of their dreams.

7. Sometimes it is the result of their experiences of higher contacts.

8. Sometimes it is the expression of their visions and revelations.

9. Sometimes it is the expression of their striving.

10. Sometimes it is the construction of an idea.

11. Sometimes it is an echo of the rhythm of the Higher Worlds.

12. Sometimes the music is the reflection of the blooming going on within their souls.

The sources of inspiration of composers are many. There are composers who help you to bloom and discover the light you are seeking. They help you to meet facets of yourself you never dreamed of.

Sometimes they pull you down into your glamors, illusions, and destructive emotions. Sometimes they even prepare your mind to commit crimes.

Music can be used to devastate your integrity or help you to build personal and universal bridges.

Chapter 13

The Source of Music

Harmonics and music emerge from the source of Infinity, from space. No one created harmonics. There is even music that is not composed by human beings, and its source is space. As the seven notes, the Seven Rays are played upon, and the music of space comes into being. The most advanced musicians, singers, and composers are those who are in tune with these harmonics or music. But their compositions are still a faint reflection of the music in space, like music played upon a broken instrument.

It is possible to hear the harmonics of Infinity upon emotional, mental, and intuitional planes and try to express in your composition the degree you are impressed by them.

The health and purification of our vehicles and chakras in our subtle bodies play a great role in bringing down the music of space.

Each composer draws the harmonics from the sphere into which his consciousness can penetrate. The harmonics take shape in our consciousness according to our visualization, creative imagination, and thoughtforms and also according to the power of our concentration.[1]

The harmonics of higher spheres demand a concentrated consciousness in that sphere in order to be clearly impressed. Lack of concentration breaks the flow and causes degeneration in transmission.

Ancient masters of music, such as in Greece and China, practiced deep meditation to be able to bring the heavenly music to earth. The harmonics in space have the power to

1. Expand our consciousness
2. Organize and integrate our mind
3. Purify our emotions
4. Heal our body
5. Create soul infusion
6. Build a communication line between us and higher spheres
7. Cause peace, freedom, and illumination within our environment

1. For help in these skills see the following books: *Mental Exercises, The Art of Visualization, The Creative Fire,* and *The Science of Meditation.*

Real composers, musicians, and singers are true healers and saviors of the race.

Every great server is an embodied music for humanity.

Music also has a very strong evocative effect on people and objects and on animals and birds. It brings out their essence and speeds their evolution. In the future, music will be used to develop virtues, such as the sense of responsibility, cooperation, trustworthiness, solemnity, etc. Music will be able to heal smokers, alcohol users, drug users, and criminals. Because of certain music, leaders of nations will be sublimated to such a degree that war will be impossible because the music will evoke love, compassion, and Intuition, which are real powers to solve problems.

A real musician first hears and then composes. He may also see beauties in the Subtle Worlds that are objectifications of harmonics. Each beauty has the possibility to turn into music.

Musicians inherit that which exists in space. If we go deeper into this fact, we discover the keys leading us to the universal Purpose, Plan, and Ideas, which are nothing else but the notes in the Cosmic harmonics.

Scientists have been telling us that the whole of existence was the result of an accident. What an unscientific statement! The understanding that there are harmonics in space erases such an illusion of a frozen consciousness.

One day it will be proven that all phenomena of Nature are objectified musical notes and chords. Even all events on earth are the result of relations of notes. The music or the harmonics in space, as we go deeper into the subject, are the architects of the Universe. But as these harmonics came down to the human mental and emotional planes, they became contaminated with our vices, ego, vanity, separatism, slander, jealousy, revenge, greed, fanaticism, lust, fear, and anger and became the music we have now. The events on earth are distorted compositions of distorted minds.

Human speech, words, even alphabets of nations are frozen notes in letters. Mantrams have such power because they cause resonance in higher spheres and let loose the energies to earth.

The greatest science in the future, as it was in the beginning, will be the science of sound, harmonics, and music. Sound will replace all our complicated machinery and devices. But this science will be given to those who will work to restore the Plan on Earth, or who are in harmony with the "purpose which the Masters know and serve."

The progress of every living form is achieved through being able to hear the music within. The whole man is a music that can turn into better and better harmonics. Eventually, sound listens to the music of its vehicles and translates the vehicles on to a higher plane of existence when this music forms one of the notes of a higher composition.

The ancients in India revealed a great secret when they stated that God sang and all Existence came into being. Thus, there is nothing else but music in process of becoming a symphony.

Those who learn the art and the science of meditation eventually will be able to learn to hear their own music and harmonize it with the song of Existence. They will penetrate into the glory of the laws and principles that perpetuate the song, and then contact the singer within themselves and within the whole.

Sound, color, and numbers are a trinity inseparable from each other. Where there is sound, there is color. Where there is color there are number and forms.

These three correspond to the three dynamics behind all manifestation.

Will	Purpose	Sound, Music
Love	Plan	Color
Light	Action	Number, Form

Chapter 14

Rhythmic Living

People think about music and dance or start drumming immediately when they hear the word *rhythm*. But we can expand this concept and think about other rhythms. Life is a rhythmic action that we cannot always notice. Many actions we repeat rhythmically—daily, weekly, monthly, or annually.

Also, our emotions follow a certain rhythm, and mental activities are very often rhythmic.

One must observe oneself to see the rhythm in his life and how he can benefit if he introduces into his life a better rhythm, a more regulated rhythm.

It can also be seen that life around us is rhythmic, and especially rhythmic in the contacts of the Subtle and Fiery Worlds. If we observe life closely, we see that our life is surrounded by a rhythmic motion. We have the opportunity to orchestrate these rhythms and improve most of them.

In our spiritual life we have the rhythm of praying, meditating, reading, and creativity. We pray daily or daily try to meditate, read, and engage in creative labor. If the rhythm of such actions is regulated, we receive great benefit from them.

Rhythm creates a condition in which transference of higher energy becomes possible. It creates a whirlpool between the physical and higher spheres through which the higher contacts the lower, bringing in energy and various blessings. When the rhythm is not kept regular, the whirlpool slowly disintegrates and vanishes. This is true especially for our prayers, meditation, study, creativity, or creative service.

Rhythm is cumulative. The benefits of rhythm accumulate, improve, and increase. If one does his regular meditation every day, in one year's time he builds those mental apparatuses that serve as transmitters for higher ideas, visions, inspirations, and revelations.

The transmission of such blessings is distorted or scattered when the rhythm is not kept or continually charged.

In creative work the time or the duration is so important. Higher forces are very rhythmic and always make themselves available in the same moment of the day or week. If the rhythm is broken, the communication and flow of energy eventually stops.[1]

---

1. See Chs. 44 and 45 on "Muses" in *The Creative Fire.*

If a pianist or violinist does not exercise rhythmically, he eventually loses his talent; if he carries on his exercises rhythmically, his talent increases. The same is true in sports. People in sports know the importance of rhythmic rehearsals, or exercises, without which they would fail.

In meditation and in creative labor, rhythm is so important. The law of rhythm is everywhere in the Universe. The evolutionary force works with rhythm. The rhythm of the Universe comes into existence when the threads of the etheric network crisscross each other, thus establishing the various rhythms in the Universe. Every rhythm is a release and inflow of energy.

In establishing a rhythmic living in our life, we synchronize with the rhythms in the network of energies, which in turn strengthen us and carry us toward greater achievements.

Our etheric centers and the centers in our subtler bodies need the coordination of rhythm, first within the body itself, then with the centers of the higher bodies.

The Chalice plays a great role in coordinating the centers through its steady rhythm.

Chapter 15

Music of Space

Music, like poetry or literature, can be of the past and present and sometimes it aspires toward the future. Most contemporary music is oriented toward the past and present; it does not have future in it. There is some music which sings for the future, but there are songs that are dedicated to the past and galvanized by hatred and anger. Such music lacks future. Improvement of life, beauty, freedom, and joy start from the beauty, freedom, and joy of the past. It is not necessary to have words depicting the future; it is the music, the voice that speaks about the future, about space.

Most of the music we hear is matter, emotions, or emotionally controlled thoughts. It speaks about the past, about the present, but does not make a breakthrough to space, the future.

It is possible to express past, present, and future in music. Future is not being used now. It is all past and present or chaos.

Music is the expression of the human psyche. If the heart and mind do not aspire and strive to something beyond, music stays on a horizontal level and does not make a breakthrough toward space. Man must strive to get out of the mental, emotional, and worldly problems to be able to make a breakthrough into space.

Space music is not nebulous, confused music that has no characteristic and no direction. It is built of various states of consciousness opened to the entrance of space.

Space music is not even the music of galaxies, constellations, and stars, which is also music of the present but not of the future. Future is related to the understanding, meaning, and significance, not to the form. Or it is music that binds you to the formlessness beyond the physical, emotional, and mental forms that surrounds us. It needs great labor to free ourselves from physical and emotional patterns and thoughtforms of the past and the present. They are the substances of our life and they use us to feel alive, but we must go beyond them toward the formless Space — toward the future.

The music of the future slowly detaches itself from old rhythms that are familiar in our physical, emotional, and mental worlds. New music is not based on old rhythms, on old melodies or measures. It has its own rhythm and measure, evocative of the future or space.

There are three major rhythms — past, present, and future. How does the future rhythm differ from the past? The consciousness conditions it, the consciousness that is established in the future.

People have been drumming the past for many centuries. When will the drumming of the future start? If music is stuck to the past, life goes on the level of the past. But the one who breaks the rhythm of the past and present becomes a pioneer, a genius, and a revolutionary in a higher sense among the multitudes.

The mind must think about Infinity, about space, free from the limitation of past worldly thoughtforms, emotional patterns, and disturbing political and social events. The mind must make the breakthrough through abstract thoughtforms, even intuitional ideas. Later the hands will obey and play music that belongs to space, to Infinity.

One can put the entire Infinity in a short melody if his mind is infused with Infinity. Actually, Infinity flows through our mind, but we are not always conscious of it. When we become conscious, we formulate it in music or words. Music is a better vehicle than words because words have more mundane associations than notes. Feeling that eternity is flowing through you is a step toward understanding Infinity.

The music of Infinity is supremely rhythmic but unlike the rhythm of average music. It has four dimensional rhythm related to the planetary, systemic, zodiacal, and Cosmic rhythms, combined together as one rhythm.

The music of Infinity is composed for transformation. In that music people's glamors, illusions, separatism, greed, fanaticism, and hatred will eventually vanish, and people will strip themselves from ugliness and non goal-fitness in order to transform themselves. This is what the music of Infinity must do. It is not a source of pleasures but a source of transformation to make earthbound people become Infinity bound souls.

The music of the spheres is a real fact, but it was presented in such a way that people thought it was wishful thinking or a miraculous phenomenon. The music of the spheres is the chords of the planets and, often, the vibration of stars.

Every heavenly body has its sound, and most of the time this sound is extremely harmonious and melodious. The sound emanates from the spirit of the planet vibrating throughout its body. And, because they are far more advanced in their evolution than human beings on this planet, these heavenly bodies emanate the most beautiful harmony that, mixing with the harmony of others, makes sometimes oceanic, overwhelming harmony and music.

Some people have heard these sounds, and this fact is recorded in history. This hearing is allowed only for one or two minutes for human beings. A little dosage of this music is a most uplifting experience, but if it continues — because of cracks in our aura and nervous system— it leads to devastation. Some psychic illnesses are the result of hearing part of this harmony.

When I refer to the music of Infinity, I have in mind the music of the spheres and also beyond our solar system, into Cosmos.

New musicians will come, and after lots of imitation they will eventually be in contact with the music of Infinity. Their compositions will open a new age of communication with Higher Worlds or a new stage of expansion of consciousness and a new relationship with other human beings.

✦

Chapter 16

Art and Music

In creative art you must try to put in as many dimensions as possible. For example, the form and color of a painting are dimensions. Space is another dimension. Meaning is another one.

If a painting presents or symbolizes a story which has many dimensions in itself, the story enriches the painting with several dimensions. When people look at the painting, the dimensions of the story behind the painting condition their responses.

Man is a multidimensional being. The more dimensions which are touched through art, the greater will be the response of man.

It is the same with music. A simple melody becomes multidimensional when it is related to or is the expression of a myth, a legend, or a story. The legend or the myth which survived for ages becomes the soul of the painting or the music. It is this soul which gives meaning and significance to the manifestation of the art.

It is also possible to orchestrate a melody or a painting or a dance with the legend or myth in such a way that the legend or myth fills the gaps existing in the art object due to its lack of perfect style. For example, you see some statues which are not sculptured by great masters, but they have a profound impression upon human beings, not because of the subtlety of the art but because of the legend or myth with which they are woven. In such cases, the art object is a door which leads you into the gallery of the legend or myth where you can find complete satisfaction.

I once saw a movie in which there was a very ugly looking character who was also the most loving and most sacrificial figure. Everybody loved him; the audience even had tears in their eyes. I asked myself why this character could not be presented with beauty? Why couldn't his inner beauty be expressed through his physical beauty? Why this effort to make ugliness be loved to such a degree that people almost identified with it?

The answer was very simple. The author of the film wanted to impress ugliness upon the minds of people through making the ugliness lovable. What an ingenious invention!

The etheric bodies of millions of people were impressed with a very disfigured form, an ugly form, and the ugliness was accepted because of the qualities of behavior the character presented.

People are not aware of how much distortion they introduce into their etheric bodies, and then they complain of ill health.

Chapter 17

My Music Teacher

I had a very old and wise Music Teacher. He advised me to observe the motion of Nature. For example, I was told to observe the

— waterfalls
— rivers
— creeks
— rain drops
— floods

He told me that there are various songs, symphonies, or melodies of Nature built not only on sound but also on rhythmic motion.

He further advised me to observe with passion the waves of oceans and lakes and notice their rhythmic motions. One day he said even to observe the motion created on the surface of a lake by an insect or a jumping fish.

On other days he advised me to observe the motion of the branches of trees, bushes, flowers in the meadows, grass on the sides of hills when under the influence of gales and tornadoes and winds of different speeds.

He advised me to observe birds moving from branch to branch or when flying in the sky, whether singly or in group formation. "Remember," he said "they are one of the instruments of Nature's symphony."

He further advised me to observe horses running and other animals, such as bulls, goats, sheep, tigers, lions, cats, dogs. My first duty was to watch their movements — to observe how they walk, run, or play.

I remember one day he advised me to observe the movements of clouds and their formations.

There is a complicated motion in Nature. Those who are interested in composing music must be soaked in the movements of Nature because the real music must reflect the movements of Nature.

He wanted me to observe various flowers and their motions. They were so different.

One morning we were in front of a high mountain from which rocks were falling into a river. We observed the falling rocks for six hours. They had a very amazing rhythm, speed, and special forms of acceleration while falling.

He recommended that I sit for six months on a corner of a street and observe how people were walking, moving their hands, heads, etc. "Through observation," he said, "it is possible to sense the rhythm of Nature and tune in with it."

I was very fond of watching kittens. When four or five of them would play with each other and with their mother, what a joy it was for me. I saw many motions, and I saw how each one was different and meaningful.

For a few years I did not see my Teacher. When we met again he asked, "Do you continue to watch motions — every kind and form of motion?" And then he added, "Now it is time to reproduce the many motions on the drum."

Then he demonstrated many motions on the drum. This was so fascinating for me. Then he took the violin and he played the music of a comet that one day he and I had watched. It was a total replica of the music of a comet. "If you want to be a musician and a composer, observe the motions of Nature."

When one watches consciously the movements of Nature, he feels energized. One day I asked my Teacher about being energized. He said every motion of Nature is an emanation of energy. Those who observe receive the energy.

I remember one day when I and some boys, students of music, observed the movements of lightning. That night I could not sleep because of the charge. Every flash of lightning had a different pattern, color, and intensity.

Once when I came to visit my Teacher in his mountain hut, he ran to the door and said to hurry and come in. He took me to his study room. From the roof drops of water were falling into two containers. "Listen," he said, "to the difference each sound makes, and notice the rhythm in the duration of each and of both together. Look at the forms they create in the container. Without a word we watched for two hours. Then he said, "Welcome. What can I do for you?"

For a few hours he spoke about the drops, and that day I understood the power of his observation. He could see almost everything. At one moment he said, "Did you notice the song of the bird in its relation to the drops and the configuration?" I told him that I was so concentrated on watching the drops that I could not hear anything else.

That is primitive concentration. "Concentration," he continued "is not exclusion but inclusion without being disturbed. All your physical ways of walking, running, moving, talking, jumping are the result of your feeling and thinking. An observing eye can read your thought through the music of your movements."

After observing motion, my duty was to observe natural colors in any form, at any place. And my third duty was to listen very carefully to the sounds of Nature — animals, birds, water, trees, rolling stones, waves, and so on. "The more you communicate with Nature, the more you discover yourself," he said.

After that day I did not see him. He climbed a high mountain for a few days and never came back.

Chapter 18

Temple Dances

According to the esoteric tradition, Temple dances originated from the Hierarchy. When the Hierarchy came to this planet, they saw that humanity was really animallike. Human beings needed rhythm, melody, music, and harmony so that they could create some kind of integration, alignment, and synchronization in their physical, emotional, and mental natures. Health, happiness, intelligence, consciousness, and energy all depend on harmony, synchronization, and rhythm. For example, if a dancer is dancing with rhythm and harmony, he generates a very beautiful rhythm and harmony in space.

In space there are lots of disturbances — short waves, long waves, gossip going on through radios and televisions. All of this chaos being poured into space creates contradictory, antagonistic forces that are always battering and annihilating each other. Every energy that is going from your mind is an entity. It may be a short lived or long lived entity. It does not have a soul, but it is animated by your etheric, astral, and mental bodies.

All these waves in space fight against each other as if they were human beings. As two opposing currents in the river, they fight against each other. Or as two different energies or forces or chemicals, they counteract each other.

We have a tremendous amount of disturbances in space, which reflects back to earth and creates this chaos in which we are living. Doctors have not considered that most of the sicknesses we have on this planet are the result of disturbances in the spheres. But they are very close to making this discovery. Many psychiatrists, doctors, and psychologists have come to the conclusion that spatial electronics or things that are in space — electrical waves, electronic waves, different currents coming from stars and galaxies — are cyclically creating manifestations of physical, emotional, and mental diseases.

Esoterically it was noticed that if a big star in space exploded, it created a tremendous amount of emotional excitement, depression, or tension. Why? It is exactly like entering into a room where there is a tremendous amount of pressure. For example, you are flying in the airplane, and the airplane is pressurized. Suddenly the pressure drops or a window is broken. What happens if you do not have oxygen masks? You die.

This pressure that is created with the explosion of a comet or star affects the brain cells, the emotions, the glands, the nervous system, everything that man is, and he feels different, unpleasant, irritated.

But all these disturbances that we have in space can be eliminated slowly if we create rhythmic physical movements, rhythmic emotional movements, rhythmic mental movements and harmonize them together and project them into space. Whatever you are doing now, the next moment it belongs to space. As soon as you think, it is gone; an energy wave is gone. It is in space. If that energy wave is really harmonious, what you are doing is creating in some part of that space a cleaning, a harmony, a beauty. Higher worlds, higher forces can only reach us through such areas that are harmonized in space.

So, the Hierarchy taught little dances: first, to synchronize, align, and integrate our physical, emotional, mental nature; second, to purify the space in which they exist.

We are dancing in this space, bringing in rhythm and harmony. We are purifying the space. That is why they are called Temple dances. Dances in the Temple make the Temple holy because all these harmonious emanations are changing the atomic structures of the things around you.

If you direct an evil thought to a piece of paper and use an advanced instrument, you will see that the evil thought is dislocating the atoms in the paper and disturbing the atomic activities in it. When the paper is disturbed by somebody reading your words, the things you are writing upon it are not exactly what you wanted to say because they are disturbed by the atomic disturbances in the paper.

That is why when you have a flower and you are talking to the flower and loving it, the flower is growing. If you are hating the flower, the flower is dying. If you love a man or woman, he or she is blooming. If you start feeling icky about a person, he droops.

What is the secret of all this? The real secret is the harmonious emanations — physical rhythm, emotional rhythm, mental rhythm — if they are synchronized and harmonized with each other and broadcast physically. This means that etherically, emotionally, mentally they create a tremendous clearing and harmonizing process in the earth. That is the foundation of the Temple dances.

The second reason for Temple dances is that they build a bridge between your personality and your Soul. Your physical body rhythmically obeys the music you are hearing. Emotionally, you are translating the musical emotion. By translating the meaning of the things you are dancing you become mentally involved. Then you see the vision and your Soul is involved. So, physical rhythm, emotions, mental thought, and vision are reaching your personality along with your Soul or Higher

Self. When you bridge — physically, emotionally, mentally — it means you are coordinated. When you are coordinated, as it is in you, so it is in the Universe. In any coordinated instrument, the higher forces have a chance to manifest themselves.

With respect to the world, it is the Hierarchy that is going to manifest. With respect to the human body, your Soul is going to manifest. When your Soul is manifested, you are bringing tremendous amounts of Beauty, Goodness, Righteousness, Freedom, and Joy into your environment because you are integrated. This is the first step.

All healing processes are nothing else but processes of creating harmony and rhythm in all the things you are — physically, emotionally, mentally. That is pure healing. You will heal yourself as much as you can by putting yourself in rhythm, in harmony. That is why at times you must close your curtains, dress in something very light, put on some music, and dance.

You will see how you will be healthy because most of your illnesses or health — physical, emotional, and mental — depend on either the congestion of the energy or the flow of the energy that you have accumulated within yourself. If you are accumulating physical, emotional, or mental energy and it is not flowing out, you are creating congestion, and this congestion will create nervous, glandular, or organic problems. But if you are radiating, you are becoming a channel for that energy. When the energy is not congested in you, you are healthy. A mind that accumulates lots of knowledge and does not know how to manifest it creatively is eventually going to be sick. The same is true for the physical body. Elimination is very important. Reception is very important. These two must be rhythmically balanced.

The second step is to make the personality integrated and whole, then to fuse it with the Soul.

The third step is interesting. Through the dance you bring great amounts of energy, and if you are really an informed and mature disciple, you can take that energy and use it for others — to heal them, to raise them, to purify them, to enlighten them, or to stop them from certain activities. You are like a dynamo charging yourself in dance. When you are creating that dance, you can accumulate the energy and then project it later, or you can immediately project it. There are two ways to use the energy: you may receive the energy and let it go, or you may accumulate that energy and then say OM and direct that energy to a sick person and heal him.

So the third step is the accumulation of energy within you, and then the use of that energy consciously after you accumulate it. This is related to all the sacred dances.

The fourth step is changing and transforming the audience, if you can. Suppose you are ten people dancing a tremendous dance. Your dance is penetrating into their aura, creating purification and expansion in their whole system.

In the fifth step, through contact with higher forces and higher centers and through giving your energies out, you prepare the foundation of expansion of consciousness. Most of you think that by going to schools, classes, and seminars, by reading books, you are really expanding your consciousness. I will tell you what you are doing: you are buying more and more furniture, and one day you will see there is no place to move in your head because it is so loaded with furniture that there is no space left. Expansion of consciousness is not information. We are talking about a totally different thing.

Q&A

Question: *How do we learn Temple dances and know what they do for us?*

ANSWER: A Teacher will teach you, and when you learn you will see the result. You will feel it in your body.

Question: *You said that sound and color are interchangeable. How does motion enter into that?*

ANSWER: The origin of sound is motion. The origin of color is motion. It is all motion and nobody knows yet what motion is, esoterically. Esoterically, motion is the moment when the spirit is becoming matter or matter is becoming spirit. That moment of interchange is motion.

That is philosophy. We do not need that now, but we will come to it later.

Question: *What about dancing at home? How do you know your movements are effective?*

ANSWER: When you learn some real dances, you will know.

There are many things that we can explain here. For example, notes that are sung flat or sharp from the notes intended are out of order, totally not good. We understand from the sounds a person makes that he does not have an ear to replicate the sounds he hears. When you are singing this way, he starts singing that way. I have had lots of experience like that in choirs. We say he has no inner ear. The inner ear is blocked.

We also understand that colors may be good colors, bad colors, or false colors. We see that, but we do not know one thing: just as there are bad colors and bad sounds, there are also bad motions.

There are also really disturbing motions and really sickening motions. If they are done, real disharmony in the group and in the audience is created. For example, imagine somebody suddenly jumping up while we are sitting here. That is disharmony. Or when we are walking rhythmically, suddenly someone starts jumping. In relation to the other movements, that is inharmonious. Then there are motions that are inharmonious within themselves.

So, if you are singing the wrong note in a choir and being disturbing, you can also disturb the harmony of the space by walking a certain way that is not rhythmic or harmonious. People have not learned that yet. It is going to come slowly. This is why in the Temples, girls and boys must walk for six or seven months. When I went to a Temple, I thought it was really crazy. Why walk? My goodness, there is so much in the walk. You can immediately see what is wrong with people by how they are walking. If you know the secret of walking, you immediately see he has kidney troubles, his knees are no good, his pineal gland is not working, the thymus is very bad. You can immediately see it in a person's walk!

As there are rhythmic movements and harmony in sound, in color, in motion, there are also rhythmic and non rhythmic positions of your body. For example, if you are sitting in certain ways, you are going to have certain sicknesses. How does one know these things? If you are sitting crookedly for three hours, you are putting one of your vertebrae out without knowing it. I am giving just rough examples. If medical people make a really thorough examination of why this man developed this sickness and they have the film, the actual film, of how he was walking, how he was sitting, how he was moving, they will see that exactly these movements were leading to the illness.

Another example is when a girl habitually slumps when she sits. Slowly you see that her breasts, her liver, and different organs are having problems because all of her structure is not in the right position. When things are not in the right position, you need a chiropractor who can put the body in good shape. What is good shape? Good shape is the shape that creates no problems. If you are walking jerkily, you are going to have certain problems that are related to that false structure. Or if you are bouncing when you walk, something is going to be wrong there, and so forth.

Well, why are you walking like that? How can you strengthen and correct it? You are going to study body dynamics. People sit with their ankle resting on the other knee. If you physiologically examine it, all the energy is going to their sex glands. The girls and boys are becoming sexually hot because of their way of sitting or their way of sleeping.

When we were in the monasteries, the Teacher used to come at night to check how the boys were sleeping. I asked him why he was checking? "You do not know why?" he asked. "Some boys are sleeping on their stomachs. They are excited all night because their organs are touching different places. When they are sleeping in different ways, different glands are stimulated."

In monasteries they teach you how to sleep, what to wear at night so that your sexual organs are not stimulated and your blood circulation is not hampered. If you really sleep comfortably, without emotional and different centers being put in action, you will be able to go out of your body and enter high places and bring greater inspirations.

Our walking is especially important. We must come back to that. For example, if you are walking on your toes, you are creating different tensions in your body and different glands are stimulated or are under-stimulated. If you are flat-footed, you are not going to get into the army. If you have been wearing a pair of shoes for a while, when you look at the soles you will see which part is worn out. You do not notice it, but three months later the shoes tell you that you are not walking really right. You are walking pigeon-toed, for instance, and the outside of the sole is totally gone while the inside is not worn at all. If you had some machine that could show you what kind of muscle tension you are creating on this side or that side, you would then understand that perfect movement is the source of perfect health.

Question: *Is it a condition in your mental body that makes you walk incorrectly?*

ANSWER: Yes. For example, you say, "I do not like her. I do not like that. I am mad. I am crazy." Emotionally you are conditioning your body structure, and you are going to pay for it.

And if this conditioning started ten million years ago, some Teacher is going to take hard actions and say, "Walk right!" And you are going to walk. When I entered into the Temple, they said, "You are going to walk from here to that wall." It was maybe one hundred feet. I walked and came back and said, "I did it." "No," they said, "you are going to walk."

Six months I walked. For the first three months I was cursing everybody in the world. Three months later I said,

"Come to your senses now. There is something mysterious here." I learned what the mystery was.

Temple dances are not for pleasure. Temple dances are disciplinary processes to create alignment within your body, between your body and Soul, and between your Soul and the audience. With this alignment you are transforming the consciousness of the audience through rhythm and harmony and also through the subjective understanding that you are giving to them. Your subjective understanding goes through the rhythm and harmony to the audience.

Other dances are for enjoyment. Temple dances are intended not only for physical development but for emotional and mental development as well. There is visualization. There is sensitivity to energy, acceptance of energy, and transmission of the energy. It is a matter of lovingness and joyfulness and freedom.

What is the psychology of the Temple dance? Listen carefully to the notes and the words. Every note of the music has to go through your body. Your body has to become the music; every note needs to be translated. If the movement does not correspond to the music, to each note, there is a blank spot. It is empty. What that really means is that something is wrong; something is not corresponding, not harmonizing.

Chapter 19

Dance of Giving Hearts

This dance is for the transmission of heart energy from the dancers to the audience and from the audience to the dancers.

1. When you are dancing, you imagine that a blue light is taken by your fingers from the sphere of your heart and thrown to the heart center of the people, and your visualization and thought energy will direct that heart energy to their hearts. Then you are taking their heart energy to you so that tremendous heart communication starts between the dancers and the people.

2. Now you are taking the heart of the earth into heaven. By so doing, you are becoming a bridge between earth and heaven, creating harmony between them. "Thy will be done on earth as in heaven." You are linking them.

3. Then you are taking the heavenly heart, the Cosmic Heart, and bringing it to earth so that you bring great ideas and visions of the future and beauty to the earth.

4. When you have brought this to the earth, then you are again taking from your heart and giving to the people and taking from the people and going away. This way, the dance creates a tremendous alignment and integration process between the people and the dancers and between earth and heaven. Everything is harmonized, peaceful, beautiful, and rhythmic; you are living. The audience will not know where this peace and harmony came from.

This is not a mere dance; it is not a performance of movements; it is beyond that. So many dancers have been taught movements. Movements are good for the etheric and physical bodies — to control them and for mental discipline. But through movements you can also project your glamors, illusions, anxieties, and irritations to the people.

But in this dance you are sending or transmitting pure heart energy. You are doing a great service, a ceremonial Holy Communion between person and person; between earth and heaven and synthesizing them. With that joyfulness you then depart.

So, through this music and dancing, you are already transforming their lives. For example, this dance will take three hours daily of practice for six months;

then you will see the result. The dance cannot be really beautiful except when the dancers are starting to transform and expand their consciousness. It will take time to translate the mystery to the people. Before that inner transformation comes, the dance will be mechanical.

Description of Costumes

The costume of "Dance of Giving Hearts" is a long silken dress that is golden-orange in color. It is closed at the neck with long sleeves fitted at the wrist. The orange color represents loving energy. A green belt is worn, and it represents the color of life. White socks on the feet mean the purity of life's direction.

✧

Chapter 20

Creativity and Dance

Temple dances must be performed with solemnity, as if one were standing in the Presence of the Most High, and then one must fuse himself with Its power. Before starting to dance, the dancer must charge himself with that Source of energy. Temple dances are created to put the dancers in contact with higher values and higher levels of consciousness, and then to have them radiate these values and levels through their rhythmic movements.

Solemnity prepares the dancer to fuse and engage himself with the Source. Without this fusion, all that he does becomes mechanical and lacks any esoteric significance. For example, in the movements for the song, "Beloved Lord,"[1] the dancer must keep his mind focused

---

1. A Sufi prayer. Music and movements created by the author.

on the Almighty Presence in order to heal his body, mind, and heart. This energy is grounded when, with humility and surrender, he touches his heart, kneels, and brings his forehead to the floor, completing the circuit between Spirit and matter.

To surrender is to stop being a separate object in the Cosmos and to become one with the whole Universe. The moment of surrender is a moment of unification with the Almighty Power, at which time the person becomes charged.

Temple dances must not be learned all at once. They carry energy and the student must go slowly so that he changes and transforms his body, heart, and mind as he learns. If a Temple dance is learned too quickly, it loads the dancer's electrical system and causes some of the fuses to blow out.

Temple dances bring in energy from higher realms, which causes purification in the dancer's vehicles. If the dance is performed slowly, the organs and glands adjust themselves to the incoming voltage. If the dance is performed in haste, the organs and glands react with negativity or rejection.

Dances must be choreographed in such a way that the movements of the dancers create harmony and rhythm instead of agitation in the aura and a flow of psychic energy. When a dance is not choreographed according to this principle, it creates exhaustion in the system and imbalance in the whole person. There are movements that channel etheric or astral energies and movements that channel mental and higher energies. One must know what he can and wants to channel.

A harmonious dance channels all of the energies involved in the right proportion, except in rare cases where an elevated being wants to channel a particular kind of energy for a specific purpose.

Congestion and exhaustion have similar effects on the body.

Movement is a form of communication, like talking. There is a language of movements. If a person's movement is not influenced by artificiality and inner conflict, his language is clear and meaningful.

The choreographer who is creating a Temple dance must also know the science of visualization.[2] Movements transmit higher energies if the dancer can visualize. Visualization is a technique through which the human soul contacts higher energies and then transmits them through his thoughts, emotions, and movements. Until one is in contact with higher centers, his movements will be a waste of time and energy and be mechanical. Visualization is the process of receiving, transforming, and directing energy.

It is advisable to dance on wooden floors or on the earth itself. Thus the circulation of higher and lower energies balance themselves. Dancing with bare feet stimulates our organs through the massage of our toes and feet. The toes are related to various glands and organs.

---

2. See booklet, *The Art of Visualization,* for a step by step approach to this process.

These regenerate themselves when they are massaged while being charged with the spiritual energies released through fusion, chanting, visualization, and movement.

The heels are connected with the three fires of the spine. These fires are charged through certain movements and contacts the heels make with the earth. It is very healthy to dance barefooted, if the ground is grass, wood, or earth. To walk in Nature with bare feet is very healing. One receives different currents of energy from different places which invigorate the body and its various organs. Running and walking through meadows, paths, or along the seashore is also very beneficial for the etheric body and physical organs.

Feet breathe; one must give his feet a chance to breathe. Sandals are better than shoes; shoes with high heels are bad for men and women but are particularly more harmful to women. Rubber-soled shoes are better than leather. Wooden shoes are the most healthy.

In Temple dancing, it is best to dance with bare feet. One has more control over his feet and also keeps his body in direct contact with the negative pole of energy.

As a person swims in the ocean by using his body movements — going forward, backward, floating, and so on — similarly through visualization one controls the substance of the mind and creates those forms that transfer special kinds of energy, or translate ideas, impressions, and inspirations which otherwise would remain too abstract. Visualization enables a person to contact those levels from which the person wants to draw energy and transmit energy.

If a person is anchored in the Intuitional Plane, he brings energy from the Intuitional Plane. If he is anchored in the Third, Second, or First Cosmic Ethers, he brings energy from those planes.

When the dancer uses visualization as he dances, he draws energy from the source into which he is anchored and radiates those energies out through the use of proper movements and gestures. Gestures are like pauses in music.

It is possible to regenerate our bodies when we are skilled in the science of visualization. Visualization enables us to control matter, substance, force, and energy. When a person's urges and drives, vices and desires, glamors and illusions want him to dream, we say that he is involved in imagination. Creative imagination is the ability to give form to one's impressions and inspirations and to direct the energy.

First, visualization is pictorial vision on the mental plane where one has the ability to create a form, hold it in his vision, charge it, develop it, and carry it toward perfection.

Second, one tries to translate higher impressions into form in order to try to understand them with the mind.

Third, through visualization, one can slowly dispense with thoughtforms and use energy formations. Thoughtforms reflect the three lower planes; energy formations reflect the Intuitional Plane and higher planes.

Motions each have their Ray. A First Ray personality or soul speaks a different language of movements than a Second, Sixth, or Seventh Ray personality or soul. The First Ray is direct, abrupt; the Second Ray is round; the Sixth Ray is a mixed configuration, described as being "sticky"; the Seventh Ray is ceremonial and floating. Through observing the mannerisms of an individual, it is possible to detect the Rays in operation.

Imagination, creative imagination, and visualization differ from each other according to the source which conducts them. For example, if the sex center, solar plexus, or physical and emotional desires and interests are creating a person's mental pictures, he is imagining. If his thoughts, ideas, plans, and goals are controlling his mental activity, he is engaged in creative imagination. If his soul is controlling the mental body and trying to translate higher impressions through visual pictures to his mind, he is engaged in visualization.

In visualization, a person's soul is imposing a new rhythm upon his personality through visual symbols or pictures, or by channeling new energies into his system. Imagination is mechanical. Creative imagination is carried on through inspiration. Visualization is conducted by will and deliberation.

It is possible for a person to see with his imagination when his eyes are closed. For example, one can see objects of sexual and material desire. This is not visualization but astral vision. In advanced schools, this is considered a sickness because the person cannot free himself from such "visions," and he often develops a heavy guilt complex or finds himself exhausted. Astral vision changes into an attack when dark forces impose various pictures and forms upon the person to drive him to insanity or to channel degenerating forces through him.

Visualization is always under control; the person has the power to see or to erase all that he sees. Imagination is carried on through the solar plexus. Creative imagination is carried on through the throat and ajna centers. Visualization is carried on in the electromagnetic field built in the head by the radiation of the pineal gland, pituitary body, and carotid gland under the direction of the head center and human soul.

Certain dietary practices are necessary to develop visualization. A diet consisting mostly of vegetables, nuts, grains, and fruits helps visualization. Meat, alcohol, drugs, marijuana, tobacco, and caffeine block the power of visualization. Loud music and noise weaken the power of visualization. Sleep and purity of contacts are very important for visualization. Excessive sexual practices even close the seeing inner eye.

Through visualization you can understand complicated mysteries. Thus, imagination, creative imagination, and visualization are ways and means to come in contact with various kinds of energies and use those energies for our upliftment and transformation — or for our degeneration and destruction.

While dancing, if you have things that are related to your lower nature in your imagination or vision, you will stimulate your lower centers and use all the generated energies for your lower centers. If you have symbols of great ideas, they will stimulate your higher nature. If you have pictures in your inner vision which are related to the mysteries of Nature, initiations, and centers, you will channel energies that will transform the world. This is why Temple dances, sacred ceremonies, and rituals that are performed with higher visualization are important.

Forms are related to four elements:

- Fire
- Air
- Water
- Earth

Imagination uses earth and water forms. Creative imagination is related to air. Visualization is related to fire.

Visualization can be done in group formation, eliminating the possible dangers of over-stimulation.

One can visualize in terms of his senses. For example, you hear a beautiful melody. You create it and you hear it, as real and alive as any music. You can orchestrate it. You can make it a solo performed by any instrument. When you see that it has become just what you want, you record it.

You can visualize form, color, and movement through your eyes. You can visualize through your touch, smell, or taste, or you can visualize through the qualities of all your senses simultaneously. Such a visualization is always equal to real creativity.

To imagine music is different from visualizing music. In visualizing music, you literally hear it. You can choose forms taken from Nature as visualization exercises, such as:

- sunrise
- hills
- snowy mountains
- trees
- waterfalls
- lakes
- rivers
- oceans

We must be careful in the beginning to avoid visualizing any form which reminds us of painful experiences or memories. We cannot always know what form will bring about such a reminder because we sometimes forget what has happened to us in the past — five years or thirty years ago. But we will know that we have chosen incorrectly if our visualization weakens us, or creates anxiety, depression, or negativity. In such cases, the chosen subject for visualization must be changed immediately.

Visualization can bring subconscious memories to the surface and cause various troubles if it is not handled scientifically. That is why we are told that our karma must allow us to work on higher levels of striving, or else our efforts will create negative results.

Through labor, service, and sacrifice; through living a life of beauty, goodness, and righteousness, one pays his karma and then is allowed to engage in higher striving.

Every movement in a sacred dance must have a meaning. All movements must be based upon the secret language of expression.

People think that animals communicate with each other through vocal expression. This is true to a certain degree, but this language is exoteric, related to outer existence. Animals also have an esoteric language formed by their mannerisms and movements. They express deeper feelings and intentions through their manners, movements, and gestures.

Thus, there is a language of movement which one may use, especially in dancing. Through dance one can express those ideas which would otherwise be very difficult to express in words. Words are three-dimensional; movement and mannerisms are four-dimensional, and even more condensed and conformed.

Before one engages himself in sacred dancing, he must first learn the language of movement, and proficiently "speak" that language.

Second, he must purify his emotions and thoughts because the dance amplifies them, strengthens them, and makes them powerful energies which will control the dancer's life. If his emotions and thoughts are not pure or constructive, they become an uncontrollable flood which will destroy his life and relationships when the energy invoked by the movements begins to flow throughout his nature. That is why in ancient Temples the dancers were supposed to be extremely pure or virgin in body, emotions, and mind.

Third, he must refine his power of visualization because it is through visualization that higher energies are contacted, translated, and transmitted to the body. In some monasteries, dancers observe various disciplines to strengthen their etheric, astral, and mental centers, preventing any short-circuit in them when the currents of energy are released into their nature.

It was also known that the dancers were collected by their soul Rays to perform dances composed in the nature of the same Ray.

In dance, there is the esoteric science of color, lighting, and forms of painting used as backdrops for dance.

Dance, or orchestrated movement, causes integration in the physical, emotional, and mental bodies, as well as a harmonious relationship between these three bodies and the human soul. Organized ceremonies, movements, or dance not only bring in energy from higher sources but also release those energies accumulated in the chakras of the threefold vehicles. Such energies can be absorbed by our bodies and expressed as vitality. This is especially true when the dance is performed by a well-coordinated group, the members of which have the same vision, striving, honesty, and love. The energies of the centers of the three vehicles of the group members are released and the accumulated release of energy from the group can bring in powerful energies for the regeneration of the world and have a great impact on the planetary centers.

Actually, if one studies the sacred dances of ancient peoples, he will discover that there were dances performed for rain, wind, a good harvest, and pleasant seasons. The ancients knew that Nature could be influenced by group dancing. Dances were also used to explain mysteries. For example, in my childhood I did not understand why we were only able to see one side of the moon. My Father took me to see a dance, called the earth-moon dance. After watching, I immediately understood this relationship. There are dances that also explain mysterious aspects in the psychology of man and the Universe.

It was very popular to express feelings and thoughts through dance and movement instead of speech. I saw a dancer express his feelings and guilt through the movements of his own dance much more clearly and deeply than words could express. In dancing, one can often express the mood of his physical body, the feelings of his emotional body, and the ideas of his mental body in a much greater potency than by singing or talking.

Animals perform certain rituals which are a form of dancing to express their urges, drives, and even their feelings and thoughts.

Dancing is also used to impress us with ideal forms of beauty, perfection, and with Archetypes. For example, I saw a dance entitled "Cooperation." What harmony of rhythm, movement, and color; what movement and diversity in unity! After seeing this dance, I grasped a deeper meaning of cooperation.

Dance is also used to dissipate accumulated evil feelings, thoughts, and intentions. Such dances are First Ray dances, often using swords and fire. The dancers are usually those who have First Ray souls. Through such dances, evil is dissipated from homes, communities, and nations. The movements, chanting, and music together with energies released from space, are specially prepared to destroy such accumulations.

Dancing develops sincerity, straightforwardness, and directness in a person's nature. Dancing makes one act grounded upon fact, not in dreams and abstractions. A real dancer wants practicality. An unreal dancer talks about abstract ideas. In old schools, Temple dances were imperative because they were used to teach disciples not to talk and lecture only, but to *live.*

Some people are lost in theory, dreams, and ideas. But dancers seek actualization. Dancing gives the gift of practicality, straightforwardness, and "down-to-earthness." This became very clear after watching the growth and development of young boys who performed Temple dances for a few years. Those who once were dreamy, abstract, and "spaced" became active, practical, down-to-earth, and realistic.

Dancers were instructed in meditation. No one can properly dance a Temple dance without being trained in the science of meditation. Meditation is like ploughing the fields of the mental plane and planting seeds for a good harvest. The seeds are taken from space, or from higher realms, and brought down to the mental plane. It is in the mental plane that the seeds will grow and bring richness and abundance to life.

As one thinks in the spirit of service and enlightenment, he tills the fields of his mind and sows those fields with seed-ideas from higher realms. The mental plane is just like the fields of the earth filled with every kind of plant life. But if one wants to cultivate those fields and use them for a specific purpose, he must plough them and help them produce the fruits he needs at a particular time.

The ploughing process is thinking in the mental fields. Then there are sowers who bring the seeds and scatter them over the fields. The sowers are the magnetic responses of higher realms which precipitate seeds of ideas, visions, and even revelations upon the fields, making them fruitful in the future.

In the process of selecting the dancers, the Teachers would determine the motives of the dancers. One of my Teachers said that motives were like a small rudder which determined the direction of a big ship. If a person's motive is selfish and separative, he will have a negative reaction toward the forces of Nature. If his motive is inclusive, selfless, and sacrificial, he is in harmony with the beneficent forces of the Universe. He does not work against these forces by creating friction or cleavages. A disciple is in tune with the Plan and the Purpose of the Great Life. The Plan and the Purpose find expression through all that the disciple speaks and does, through all his thoughts and motives.

There are different stages of dancers. There is the dancer whose body is in harmony with the music. There is the dancer whose body is in harmony with his emotions. There is the dancer whose body is in harmony with his thoughts while he dances. There is the dancer whose body is not only harmonized with his emotions and thoughts but also with his visions.

There is a great difference between a dancer and a disciple. A dancer may dance to any music with any motive, obeying his own will. A disciple dances in the light of the Will of the Father. The disciple does not belong to himself; when a order comes to him, he obeys. Disciples do not exist for themselves.

Lao Tse once said, "The greatest value of a window is in its opening." The greatest value of a dish is its emptiness. The greatest value of a door is its open space. If you are a closed window, you are standing in the window as your own barrier. If your separative self is absent, you are one with space, and there are no cleavages within you because, in essence, you are space. You cleared away all that separates you from the One Self.

Man exists only because of those elements in him which separate him from the One Self. Once these elements are wiped away, he lives, moves, and has his existence as space, as the One Self.

The Dweller on the Threshold is a closed door; you closed your True Self with the not-self. You are the greatest barrier on your own path. If you remove your barrier, which is the personality or the element of separatism, your door opens and you enter your own Infinity.

Finally, sacred dances are instrumental in bringing Divine Will to earth. In sacred dances, music is the Divine Will manifesting as Purpose. The dance is the Plan, which actualizes the Purpose and makes it tangible. Unless one dances, he cannot understand the Purpose of his life. This means, unless one fulfills the Plan, the Purpose cannot be revealed.

When a Purpose lives according to the Plan, Divine Will manifests. To dance means to harmonize or synchronize all your thoughts, emotions, words, and actions with Divine Will.

In sacred dancing, the dancers represent physical, emotional, and mental vehicles. When they learn through a labor of ages to harmonize themselves to the music, to the Purpose — to live a purposeful, meaningful life — the Divine Presence in them emerges in Its whole beauty.

Chapter 21

Temple Dances and Music

Sacred dances were given by Teachers of humanity for specific purposes:

1. To create a closer integration between the physical and etheric body, between the physical-etheric body and the astral body, and between all these and the mental body

2. To stimulate certain centers in the etheric body

3. To develop the astral body

4. To put people in contact with energy sources in the Universe

5. To make people serve others, by transmitting certain constructive energies accumulated and distributed by the dance

The people living on this planet eighteen million years ago were very primitive. They lacked coordination between certain parts of their mechanisms. They were mechanically driven for the most part by hunger, sex, and fear, and they were also put into motion by certain entities living in the etheric and astral planes.

The Teachers of humanity wanted to hasten its evolution, and one of Their techniques was to use sacred dances. Dances were different at that time; they were done in slow motion with much repetition and few words. They were often monotonous with strong variations of notes.

The first kind of dance that was presented was *Hatha Yoga*. Hatha Yoga dances were slow dances performed very ritualistically. They entailed forty-nine major postures designed to assist the etheric and physical bodies to coordinate and integrate. These dances were given to humanity by advanced Teachers who were able to see clairvoyantly the effect of the various *asanas*, or the effect of the dance, on the chakras and ganglia.

We are told that the Teachers used Hatha Yoga to teach humanity for one million years, until humanity reached a state of physical-etheric coordination. Those who graduated from Hatha Yoga entered the higher school of *Bhakti Yoga*. These were ritualistic, slow dances colored with aspiration and devotion. The purpose of these dances was to make people express their emotions and share them with others.

The dances of Bhakti Yoga were used to develop worship and reverence for human beings, Nature, and natural phenomena such as trees, forests, bushes, waterfalls, mountains, lightning, rainbows, and so on. Higher classes in Bhakti Yoga were dedicated to the worship of the sun, moon, stars, and those superhuman entities who were invisible to the etheric vision of the people. Tradition says that heavenly hosts used to join in such dances with infant humanity.

Those people who were able to graduate from Bhakti Yoga where invited to a higher university, where they learned the dances of *Raja Yoga*. Raja Yoga dances were composed upon geometrical formations and rhythmic movements that were measured exactly and danced in strict configurations. Such geometrical configurations were developed to express symbols, ideas, and abstract concepts.

Each dancer was expected to go through strenuous exercises, to remember movements, and to keep his place in the group while in the meantime trying to live and express the symbols and ideas upon which the dance was constructed.

Some dances were the synthesis of these three dances, expressing rhythm, movement, chanting, devotion, and mental polarization. Of course, all three types of dances were performed through artistic development, with various musical instruments and music, color, costuming, lighting, and so on.

One who travels to the Far East and witnesses dances in remote villages cannot help but admire the costumes, ornamentation, and symbols used in their dances.

Those who were able to graduate from such training were invited to enter the study of Temple dancing. This school consisted of highly developed dancers. The dancers were required to have very beautiful and coordinated bodies, emotions, and minds. Their morals were pure, their hearts were sensitive, and their minds were disciplined.

The reason for this was that Temple dances were generally performed to transmit energy from higher centers in man, in the planet, solar system, and even beyond. One should be able to transmit such energies released from Temple dancing without hurting his physical, etheric, astral, and mental mechanisms.

Another requirement was that the dance should be performed only before a special audience ready to receive these energies and use them for constructive ends. No one was fully exposed to a Temple dance if the great Teachers were not convinced that the person was pure and would not be endangered by the released energies.

All of the dances taught by these Teachers conveyed the science of expression — how to express emotions, thoughts, ideas, moods, visions, aspirations, joy, and sorrow through movement, voice, facial changes, eyes, and so on. This art of expression required very sensitive coordination between the physical, nervous, emotional, and mental systems.

Temple dancing took a higher step when it taught how to align the physical, emotional, and mental bodies with the human soul so that he could use the bodies and dance through them — not as a body but as a soul.

Many Great Ones passed through this training and learned these sacred Temple dances. Even Jesus was a "dancer." He danced as a victorious soul before the moment of crucifixion.[1] Developing alignment and synchronization between the bodies and soul, the Teachers of humanity produced highly evolved human beings who, in their turn, served as kings, queens, teachers, and leaders of nations and humanity.

Occasionally the Teachers of humanity, upon seeing that the majority of people had graduated from certain dances or training, would withdraw the science of that dance and emphasize the dance that was still needed by humanity.

For example, Hatha Yoga is now obsolete, and the science and art of this dance has been withdrawn, leaving only the skeleton. Hatha Yoga is so old that there is hardly anyone at present who needs it. Those who continue to practice it in its deformed and obsolete form pay heavy prices for it with their ill health and even deeper side effects.

Temple dances are taught only by qualified masters. Emotional and mental dances still exist in some brotherhoods, such as the Sufi Brotherhood. But Temple dances are very hidden and only those who are qualified find their way to those locations where real Teachers can be found to instruct them.

---

1. For more information, please refer to *Christ, The Avatar of Sacrificial Love*, pp. 130-134.

Teachers of Temple dance usually know how to play a variety of instruments and know the art of dancing. Most of them are also clairvoyant, and they use this power to select those who are able to learn the dance or who enjoy watching the dance.

The three goals of Temple dancing are

- to contact or receive energy
- to assimilate that energy
- to radiate or share that energy

Remember that impressions coming from higher sources are energies. Inspiration coming from our own divine nature or from certain centers in space is energy. Ideas are energies; visions are energies; the Hierarchical Plan is energy. There are also those energies that bring new culture and new civilization, new religion, new science and art, and so on.

Those who are going to dance must know that when energy is contacted through the dance, that energy will increase the ego, vanity, separatism, and lower desires if these qualities exist in the nature of the dancer. If there are cleavages in the nature of the person, those cleavages will increase. If the dancer is not healthy, his health will deteriorate. If he has mental problems, they will increase. If his wife or girlfriend is not pure enough and he has relations with her after contacting the energy source, his presence will stimulate her weaknesses and even make her hostile toward him.

When the dancer assimilates the energy, he must be able to use that energy in creative, sacrificial service. When invoked, energy burns its container if it is not properly shared with those who are ready for it. Sharing requires strict discrimination. One must undergo a long period of training to learn how to share his energy or dissipate it in case he has no outlet for service.

Sacrificial service, hard labor, wandering in the deserts or mountains, climbing hills or engaging in creative or heroic labor may dissipate the accumulated energy.

The Hierarchy called many Teachers back for "refreshment," or rest, seeing that because of the present condition of humanity, such dances would create turmoil. There are still a few locations around the world where Temple dances are taught to a few consecrated people. Those Teachers remaining in the world are ordered to be very careful in teaching Temple dances.

Difficulties also arise from the fact that Temple dances require at least 49, 77, or 105 people to be performed properly. To bring such a qualified number of people to one place is almost an impossibility in this age. Of course, millions are ready for other kinds of dancing, but not for Temple dances.

Temple dances also require a special climate, special silence, natural beauty, retreat, contemplation, and exercise. Because of this, some Temple dances were given in remote mountain monasteries to specially trained students.

My Teacher once prohibited us from dancing. When we asked for a reason, he said, "Three miles from the monastery I saw a settlement of five hundred people who are on a pilgrimage. We may charge them prematurely if we continue dancing while they are in the area."

Temple dances were used to heal the sick. Dancers knew the secret of following the energy and sending it to the soul of the sick person. Then the energy was used to build a shield around him to prevent psychic attacks or to expel the obsessor or possessor who was making him sick. The energy was then sent to destroy the accumulations of maya, which are forces crystallized in the etheric body especially around the sacral center, and to destroy crystallized glamors, desires, crystallized thoughtforms, negative motives, and so on.

Healing dancers were highly trained to perform this sensitive and delicate surgery and to protect the patient. As a result of their dancing, many were healed, released, and freed. Those whose time was over, passed away in peace because of the sacred dances.

I once observed a dance performed in Africa by witch doctors who were trying to heal a sick person. They used the format of ancient dances; even their rhythm and drums were orderly. But they were dancing emotionally and with their body, and the energy they collected was emotional-etheric energy. If the sickness was in the etheric or astral body, there was a possibility of healing the person. But apparently the origin of the sickness was in the mental body, and they were not able to bring in mental energy because of their level of ignorance and lack of professional training. They could not help the patient; instead the patient became worse and died, surprising all who were watching, including the dancers.

Certain dances were created to spread the energy of blessings — to bless the four corners of the earth, above, below, and inside; to bless all of Nature and all living beings; to bless special people who were ready to dedicate their lives for a great task.

Dances performed for blessing need contact with the source of a higher energy — to coordinate your subtle nature and remove all barriers to make the flow of energy possible, and to choose the agent of distribution. The agent of distribution can be your hands, your eyes, your breath. In choosing the person to bless, you must be sure that he is worthy of the blessing.

This was all done ceremoniously, ritualistically, with subtle movements. The energy was then passed to the candidate for use in his higher labor. The dance performed before the blessing is an act of contacting and accumulating energy.

Ceremonies and rituals seen in certain churches are shadows of these dances of blessing. For example, the performance of baptism, matrimony, or burial services are the remains of ancient dances. Those who have eyes can see the dance behind such services. Unfortunately, some groups rejected certain rituals and ceremonies conducted in the Catholic and Orthodox churches which still express immense beauty and magnetism.

Temple dances were also performed to enlighten people. Such a dance is very powerful, accompanied by magnificent movements, music, and chanting, which wipes away the ignorance sitting in the hearts of people and evokes the light that is dormant in their hearts. These dances also reveal mysteries in man and in the Universe.

For example, a dance revealed the secret of the moon to me. I was fifteen years old and did not know why we could only see one side of the moon. The dance was so beautiful and scientifically performed that the movements of the solar system, the sun, the planets, the earth, and the moon were precisely represented by the dancers, revealing why we could see only one side of the moon.

I also saw a dance of the Seven Rays, with forty-nine dancers participating. The seven colors and their combinations used in this dance were beyond human imagination. From this dance I came to understand how certain Rays of the Seven Rays are active, while others are passive. I understood the rhythm and cycles of the Rays. It was a dance of illumination.

There were dances to reveal the mystery of the human soul and the Solar Angel, the Chalice, the Spiritual Triad, and dances of death and rebirth. Such dances were direct methods of illumination. A person can read ten books about such mysteries and still remain confused, but one dance can enlighten him.

Deeper layers of enlightenment are achieved when a person dances. If the dancer occasionally changes his role in the dance, the entire mystery stands revealed to him through the dance.

I noticed that those who were selected to perform Temple dances were very beautiful, very handsome people. They were ones who had traveled to different places on the earth to teach the Ageless Wisdom and various other arts and sciences because of their integrity and alignment with higher centers of energy.

Certain Temple dances are reflections of the dances going on in the human psyche, though man is ignorant of them. The outer dances open our eyes to see the mysterious dance taking place within.

Dancing creates magnetism, radioactivity, and focus. A dancer or group of dancers creates a field of magnetism that attracts various precious elements, Rays, impressions, ideas, and visions. It even attracts those who are going to help in the sacrificial and heroic labor for humanity.

Radioactivity clears the path, burns away obstacles, energizes beneficial elements, and releases those entities or persons who are enslaved in certain ways. Focus creates power, clarity, certainty, and simplicity. Focus synthesizes energies and releases them with a powerful impact.

There were also dances that revealed how maya, glamor, and illusion work; how subconscious urges and drives affect our life; how they are controlled and annihilated; and how posthypnotic suggestions work.

The dramatic presentation of the entire psychic domain in man was presented in dance. This was done in such a way that the audience was able to understand the mysterious life going on within themselves without their awareness.

I often wondered who the originators of these dramatic dances were. What great psychologists and artists they were to have created such masterpieces of dance.

One should not only watch such dances with utmost attention but should also participate in them to learn and understand the mystery and message of the dance, as well as experience the flow of energy, the field of magnetism, and the focus created within himself and around himself. One must feel how the higher energy passes through his body, emotional, and mental realms and how his heart feels extreme joy.

Temple dancing uses precise geometry. There is real contact with energies; there is the art of assimilation and the science of distribution through focus.

One day while we were dancing in the garden, a man commented to our supervisor that we looked like "a few chickens and a goose."

There was a thief who was sneaking into the monastery and occasionally stealing our livestock. Every week we lost a few chickens or other animals. Finally, a general meeting was held to discuss what to do about the thief. There were many propositions put forth as to how to handle him. After the discussion was over, our dance Teacher spoke against all that had been proposed and said, "If you can catch the thief and bring him to me, I will change his nature." Someone from the audience asked, "What dance can a thief do?" The Teacher answered, "If you had danced a few times with us, you would not ask such a question."

It was finally decided to catch the thief. A few people slept outdoors near the walls and gates. One day, the thief was caught and taken to our dance Teacher. He was a young boy about eighteen years old, very handsome and intelligent. He was very scared and did not know what to do. He was aware that he could be killed and burned without leaving a trace.

The dance Teacher asked him if he wanted to dance. Surprised by this question, he replied, "But I never dreamed in my life...." The Teacher gave a very mysterious look and smiled. "I will teach you, if you are a good boy and do not force us to take disciplinary action against you. As you know, you have been guilty of stealing for a long time. But we are not talking about your past; we want to create a new man out of you. Would you like to dance?" "Yes," the boy answered in surprise. "Then take off your jacket, and do as I do."

The music began with drums, wind pipe instruments, and santur. It was so exciting. After dancing certain movements for a few minutes, the boy covered his eyes with his palms and began to cry. "What is the matter?" asked the Teacher. "I feel ashamed," he said. "That is an excellent sign, but do not think about your past. We are joyful people here, and you will be one of us if you work hard enough."

After dancing for one hour, he was released and invited to stay in the monastery under the watchful eyes of the guards. He stayed one month and danced every day. We loved him so much. He was sincere, open, but always shy and ashamed. He became a good dancer.

One day he disappeared. We searched for him several hours and concluded that he had escaped from the monastery. The dance Teacher said, "Do not worry; he will not be the same boy." Six months later he visited the monastery with his younger brother and sister. They stayed in the monastery. By the time I finally left the monastery, they were the best dancers, students, and musicians. Our dance Teacher was so proud of proving that sacred dances could change human nature when prisons, the police force, and the courts could not.

A Temple dance is beauty in operation. Temple dances can change human nature because they put you in contact with your Higher Self and with higher sources of rhythm, harmony, and beauty. Temple dances also increase your psychic energy and your vitality as a whole.

Knowing this, some people misused and manipulated this idea to create military music under which the soldiers were charged and made ready to fight. Many races used such a method, charging their soldiers with trumpets, drums, or both. The intention was to mobilize the soldiers and make them kill. Military music releases a tremendous amount of adrenaline into the system, excites the solar plexus, creates revenge, and forces you to fight.

Unfortunately, some of the "classical music" written by famous people is nothing more than orchestrated military music which has penetrated into the bones of humanity for many centuries. Wars are the results of such music. This will be proven in the future when the trance and fever of killing people stops and people have a chance to think and observe scientifically, and with sanity.

Humanity has a tendency to use its knowledge for hatred, jealousy, and fear. Atomic energy was used with the same psychology — to destroy hundreds of thousands of innocent lives. Knowledge is always dangerous in the hands of those who are not purified from the six vipers of fear, anger, hatred, jealousy, revenge, and treason.

Temple dances were eventually withdrawn because the Teachers of humanity, seeing the conditions of life, decided that it would be too dangerous to reveal any further the science of dance, movement, sound, and color.

People are energized through various ways, according to the unfoldment or over-stimulation of their centers. Centers that have unfolded have the capacity to control the current of energy imparted to them. Overstimulated centers absorb all the energy directed toward them and cannot exercise any control over it. When energy is not controlled, it becomes a destructive agent.

Some dances impart energy into the sex center, solar plexus, base of spine center, or into the heart, throat, and head centers. Before such energies are released, the dancer must go through a process of purification. For example, it must be proven that he does not live in sexual fantasy or in a life of prostitution, that he has no evil motives or plans in his heart, and that he is quite free from ego and vanity.

There are movements that are not dances that can help people free themselves from certain physical, emotional, and mental habits or hindrances. Because dancing increases energy, one must have control over his mechanism to be safe.

Sacred dances were also used to promote bountiful crops from the gardens and orchards. Trees and vegetables love music and dancing. Temple dances create the right psychic atmosphere through which the right chemistry of forces is provided to trees and vegetables. If the Temple dance is performed in a garden, a miraculous growth and vitality in the garden will result.

Temple dances not only transmit energy, but they also regulate the chemistry in the neighborhood of gardens and orchards, repelling all those forces or influences that are dangerous to the plants.

Certain dances were performed during the time of the new and full moons to attract, regulate, and channel beneficial energies into the environment. Certain dances were performed at the equinoxes, or at sunrise and sunset. A beautiful Temple dance is a prayer, meditation, and contemplation. The day will be different if a dance is performed at sunrise; the night will be different with a dance at sunset.

Sometimes dancers show symptoms of fatigue and develop certain mysterious pains in their bodies, or go through a period of emotional and mental tension. This happens when the group of dancers, trying to transmit energies and prevent pollution, acts as a refinery in a physically or psychically polluted atmosphere. Such uncomfortable periods are understood and handled with gratitude because the dancers were informed that such experiences are the signs of their sacrificial service for humanity.

Dancers recover miraculously once they discharge the poison and they dance again. This is why Temple dances need highly purified personalities.

Dances performed during the most outstanding full moon, the full moon of Taurus, bring extra-planetary energies to humanity and distribute them to highly advanced and purified individuals. Such a dance is performed by Great Ones. Every movement and dance at the full moon of Taurus is a scientifically formulated device to draw energy from various constellations and stars.[2]

The group of Great Dancers receives these energies, transmits them to Their own Ashrams, and then from the Ashrams they are distributed to various parts of the world for a new, regenerative process.

---

2. For further information, see *Symphony of the Zodiac*.

Chapter 22

The Dance of Labor

People in the Far East, the Middle East, and various parts of Europe and America sing and move in certain ways as they work at various jobs. In big factories, in Nature among the forests and rivers, at the ocean, in the streets, people sometimes sing in groups as they work, as if their work were part of a dance. And, if the songs and slow movements were taken away, you would see their joy and source of energy stop. People instinctively know that certain movements and songs enable them to work longer hours in heavy labor.

There was a bakery whose six employees used to sing all day as they made the bread, put the baked goods in the display cases, and packaged the goods in boxes for customers. It was a great joy for me to visit that bakery and buy bread from that shop. Everyone was happy. It was as if they were all dancing the whole day in solemnity and focus.

The human voice and happiness during singing and working transmit a great amount of energy into the work, which also goes into the product. Unfortunately, instead of this, we now have television and radio imposing themselves and taking away the joy of singing and ecstatic movements.

People used to chant verses from holy scriptures, sing parables or mantrams, and electrify the entire atmosphere of their work place, thus preventing any temptation to express words of ingratitude, gossip, negative emotions, cursing, and so on. This kept everyone's mind on high level subjects and charged the muscles and nerves with high level energy accumulated during the focused singing and movement.

In such a mood, laborers carried out their jobs at a common pace and did not cheat the authorities because they believed that every job was given to them by the Most High and that to labor was an expression of gratitude to the Most High.

Once you are convinced that there is a conscious Source that is present behind such behavior, a source that formulated and initiated the practice of sacred dancing, you will begin to see that all over the world there is factual evidence that the Hierarchy formulated these movements and then presented them to humanity to help its evolution.

Labor was called *Karma Yoga*. This means to achieve unity with higher principles through labor. Labor was not performed for the sake of labor, nor for the sake of its results. Labor was performed to reach spiritual perfection, spiritual transformation, and initiation into higher states of consciousness and beingness.

Sacred dances were used for sacrificial acts. People used to dance and sing while they offered gifts of fruit, animals, crops, precious objects, and so on to the Most High. In certain countries, there are harvest rituals, very solemn dances in which gratitude is offered to the forces of Nature. There are rituals and ceremonies during the harvest and festivities to enjoy the fruits of the harvest.

Certain monasteries presented a young boy or girl to the Most High as a servant of light, love, and beauty through the use of sacred dancing and chanting. Acts of renunciation and detachment were also consecrated through dance and song.

At present, such dances are disappearing under the pressure of disco, rock, belly dancing, and other unmeaningful, purposeless dancing, which are excellent ways to waste energy and fall into traps that excite the lower centers.

There are dances performed for those on the verge of dying. Family members and friends began to sing and dance when it was evident that the person was leaving his body. Some of the words to these songs are very beautiful.

May light be with you.
May your path be strewn with flowers.
May the angels accompany you on your journey.
May your soul meet the Beloved.
Do not worry about us.
All will be taken care of by the Beloved.
We will come and meet you.
We will meet again in different places on Earth.
May the Most High receive you in His many mansions.

These were just a few of the verses. I attended such funeral dances with a great feeling of freedom and joy. The nature of the participants contained no grief, pain, or suffering but only joyful acceptance of the laws of life and death. During such dances, flowers were used or rose oil. The person would pass away hearing songs of joy, with pleasant fragrances and music, and enter into the next dimension of his life. In the near future, special artists will appear and rejuvenate such dances and rituals with great beauty and make them acceptable to the masses.

There were also dances performed to welcome a new baby at the time of birth. A baby born in joy, music, and dance becomes a different kind of person than one born in resentment, grief, hatred, loneliness, rejection, and fear. Some of the words sung at such an occasion are very inspiring:

We welcome you as a gift of the Most High.
You will be a servant of light,

A servant of Beauty,
A warrior for the rights of others.
You will be a carrier of the fire
And the Will of the Most High.
Blessings to your most Beautiful Mother and Father.
They will watch over you until you stand on your own
Welcome, gift of the Most High.

Can you imagine what the feelings of the soul of a baby greeted with such words would be, and what the psychological effects of such a dance would be?

It is possible to learn a sacred dance, but then perform it mechanically. The purpose of a sacred dance, however, is not in the movement and music but in its spirit. If the dance lacks the proper spirit, everything becomes mechanical. It is then a dance of the physical body through which emotions and personal thoughts are transmitted. But the objective of a sacred dance is to transmit the Spirit — the joy, gratitude, ecstasy, and the energy of Higher Realms. This can be achieved if the dancer not only knows about songs, music, words, and movements but also is spiritually elevated and absorbed into higher spheres, into higher values, causing transformation within all his personality. Unless this is done, the dancer could radiate his vices, illusions, glamors, and inner pollution and contaminate people with his lower forces. The sacredness of a dancer is his power.

Sacredness means being devoted to a special purpose, with utmost purity and focus. In ancient Temples, the dancers were called "virgins," which referred not only to their physical virginity but also to the purity of their emotional and mental bodies and to the absence of karmic debts. Only such people were allowed to dance around the sacred fire in the Temples, transmitting spiritual energies for the healing and transformation of the entire audience.

Imagine such groups of dancers, musicians, and singers who could uplift a huge audience to higher dimensions of consciousness, kindle striving toward perfection in them, and literally purify their hearts and minds.

Instead, we now have thousands of dancers intoxicated by drugs and alcohol, dancing in huge halls all over the world until morning, with sexual heat and excitement, and failing to take one step forward on the path of evolution. Some of the songs they sing and dance suggest carelessness, death, hatred, and anger and evoke intense blind urges and drives.

Young people become victims of such atmospheres and lose their sacred path. Psychic contamination and obsession begin after one attends such a dance. Sometimes these dances destroy the highest principles that a person once had in his nature.

Sacred dances were performed in ancient Egypt, China, Mongolia, and Japan. Traces of these dances still remain in traditional dances currently performed. These dances have an uplifting effect on the audience.

It is a fact that a continuous dance is being staged day and night in our body. Internal organs, the intestines, glands, lymphatic system, circulatory system, brain, heart, and cells all move continuously as a symphony, each part in harmony with the other. Science will one day be able to illustrate the internal dance that often is conducted by our desires, negative or positive emotions, glamors, illusions, higher visions, ideas, and inspirations. But the fact is that we are either in a slow or fast dance, and because of our dance and "aliveness," we influence our environment. Because our internal and external movements are orchestrated by our desires, emotions, and thoughts, how much more important it is to have lofty aspiration, emotions, and thoughts with corresponding movements in our bodies!

It is a fact that our desires, emotions, and thoughts either pollute or destroy our bodies or transform, heal, and energize our bodies. If we understand such principles, we can understand why our dancing must be orchestrated by lofty visions, ideas, and thoughts, with great joy and bliss.

We must not think that dancing is related to our physical body alone. There are also mental dances, which are movements of thoughts, ideas, and visions. Emotional dances are dances of lofty emotions, aspirations, and so on. Spiritual dances are ceremonies and rituals of the human soul to come in contact with higher sources of light, love, and beauty. A perfect dance is the combination of our fourfold nature — physical, emotional, mental, and spiritual.

Each of our bodies emanates certain radiations that affect the corresponding bodies of others. Physical movements emanate etheric waves. Emotional movements emanate waves corresponding to the emotions we express. Mental movements radiate thought waves charged with various colors according to their level and the form of our thinking.

Together these emanations leave the atmosphere of our body and saturate space, reaching the audience during the time of a performance. The effect of our dancing on others is determined by the content of our emanations, or in other words by how we think, feel, and move.

Each of our lives is a dance. If we dance a sacred dance, we will transmit beneficent energies to the world that will evoke goodness and beauty from others. If we dance with emanations of vanity, ego, separatism, illusion, fear, anger, hatred, jealousy, and revenge, we will fill the atmosphere with pollution.

An individual's life is what he gives to others. Karma is the answer to what you gave to the world. Sacred dances were created to teach humanity how to radiate and build a wonderful future for itself. Sacred dances were created to teach us how to think lofty thoughts, have fragrant emotions, and manifest them through our dances and in our daily life.

When one first begins to dance, he has no coordination between the music and his movements, emotions, and thoughts. After a few months, he learns how to control his movements to a certain degree and how to express joyful, positive emotions through them. If he continues year after year, he learns how to coordinate his movements, emotions, and thoughts with the music to express beauty and rhythm.

This is exactly what happens to the dance of our life. An aspirant cannot dance in harmony with the music and Purpose of life. A disciple begins to strive and, with strenuous efforts, coordinates his life to the Purpose of life. An initiate begins to coordinate all of his expressions with the Purpose of life. As he continues to advance, initiation after initiation, his life becomes a perfect expression of the Purpose of life.

Great Ones tell us that when They watch the "videotape" of our lives on earth, from the time of our individualization to the stage of liberation, They see how our living — or dancing — slowly improves, passing through various crises, and eventually entering into the rhythm and harmony until our whole life becomes the manifestation of the Purpose of life, gradually growing in beauty and glory.

Every day of our life is a dance — a crazy dance, full of chaotic movements, or a coordinated dance, full of beauty. Every one of us must learn how to choreograph our dance of life. Every life is a period of dancing. We must learn how to choreograph not only a day's dance but also the dance of an entire life — in such a beautiful way that we do not embarrass ourselves and disrespect or pollute our audience with ugly movements, noise, and disorder. Thus, those who learn how to dance a sacred dance also learn how to live a consecrated life which brings beauty and joy to the world.

There are dances that bring energies from zodiacal signs during each full moon. Each constellation has a different Ray, which means a different kind of influence. Through sacred dancing, these energies are attracted and expressed by the dance. This is why great Teachers want us to celebrate or observe full moons through certain disciplines, reading, and meditation, so that in the future we will be ready to dance the sacred dances, bring energy consciously from each sign of the Zodiac, and thus serve humanity.

As one purifies and makes himself ready to participate in a sacred dance, he must also consecrate himself to be able to dance the dance of life. Each improvement in our physical, emotional, and mental realms is a step of preparation toward the day when we will be able to dance with the Initiates and great Ones, thus serving the Purpose of life.

Chapter 23

The Language of Dance

Each movement in sacred dances is a word that is charged with the fire of emotions and with the direction of thought. Every dance is a form of conversation. Your conversation can be a curse or a blessing, depending on the way you perform your dance and on which level of consciousness and beingness you perform your dance.

If the movements are not created and orchestrated by one who knows how to dance, how to live a purposeful life, he cannot produce the choreography of a sacred dance. Each movement releases certain energies; it uplifts, destroys, balances, creates, regenerates, or annihilates. One must know the language of the movements.

There are seven divisions of movement:

1. straight
2. circular
3. parallel
4. triangular
5. square
6. half-circle
7. mixed combinations

The movements are also words which express thoughts, moods, dreams, visions, negative or positive emotions, or the names of natural objects. It is a difficult language that the subconscious and super-consciousness know. If the language spoken through the dance has meaning, we like the dance; if it imparts higher ideas, we fall in love with that dance. But if that dance is meaningless chatter, hallucination, or babbling, one feels depressed or ill, even if that dance is accompanied by good music, color, and lights.

A genius in the art of dance instinctively knows this language, and he choreographs each dance in such a way that the dance speaks a grammatically correct language, a language that imparts higher ideas and lofty thoughts.

The language of dance is a universal language spoken only upon the Intuitional Plane, or in a state of super-consciousness. But everyone intuitively understands it. In observing certain facial expressions or gestures, we see that they sometimes say things that could not be thoroughly explained in writing.

There are movements that are physical; others are emotional, mental, or spiritual. Each language is different, and dances are choreographed according to the level of the audience and to the purpose of the dance.

Also, movements of the body — legs, arms, neck, and head — are used to dissipate energy, collect energy, or destroy certain etheric, emotional, or mental formations existing in one's own aura or projected by the environment. These movements in turn help

- to direct energy
- to focus energy
- to circulate energy
- to stop energy

Often such movements are accompanied with a loud and sharp voice because the voice or sound charges the movement with will energy. In certain dances, such movements are performed with swords, which conduct a great amount of will energy.

To draw energy into your dancing from the etheric body, you must perform the appropriate movements. To draw energy from the emotional body, you must use your imagination. To draw energy from the mental body, you must visualize. To draw energy from your soul, you must contemplate. These techniques are used by great geniuses when they dance, and they transform the audience and uplift it into new states of consciousness.

After it is performed, a dance lives in space as an entity that is built and projected there by the audience. The more integrated the audience is, the longer the dance will live. A perfect dance is one that is composed of etheric, astral, mental, and spiritual elements.

One day in the monastery, our Teacher called three of us and said, "In the village a gala party is going to be given. One thousand people will be there and there will be music, dancing, food, and drink. I am sending you to see if you can keep the level of your consciousness while you observe the party. Then bring your conclusions to me."

The three of us took our horses and went to the village. We arrived a little late, and people were already engaged in the festivities, drinking, eating, talking, and dancing. At first it was difficult for us to observe because the power of the party was overwhelming; we were drawn to the food and dancing. But gradually we felt the stupidity of everything going on there, so we climbed up onto a balcony and observed the people with detachment.

It seemed as if we were watching people in an asylum. People were laughing, yelling, dancing, kissing, drinking, acting very silly with no purpose or beauty. Everything eventually became so disorganized that the band of musicians began fabricating music, and people were only making those movements that were easy for them to make. All were heavily drunk. Some of them were kissing; others were pouring wine on people's

heads. When things got really out of hand, we jumped back
on our horses and returned to the monastery, arriving at
three-thirty in the morning. Later that morning, our Teacher
invited us to breakfast and asked our opinion of what we
saw at the party. We gave him the list of our observations:
conflict, insanity, chaos, and so on. After a long silence,
the Teacher said, "How you observed the party is how Great
Ones observe humanity. The life that is going on in politics, education, religion, and economy is like that party.
What good can one expect from such a party? A really
good party would have good musicians and conscious dancing. If this is not observed, all is going to end in chaos."

Someday, perhaps, humanity will come to understand
that in each movement we make, we create a dance. When
we

— think

— visualize

— imagine

— talk

— move

— walk

— travel

— labor

we are putting together the elements of a great dance.
There are dances of thought, dances of human emotion,
of dreams, aspirations, devotion, dedication, worship,

and ecstasy. All human expression on all levels form the "master dance" of the human life. The value of a human being is how he dances the dance of life.

If we are one day able to see the colors and forms that our thinking creates in space, if one day we are able to see the colors, energy waves, and forms that we create in space when we talk, sing, labor, run, and walk, then we will understand that the whole expression of our nature is a dance.

Each dance must consist proportionately of four elements: etheric, emotional, mental, and spiritual. A great dance is a balance of these four elements. If these elements are not proportionate to each other, they create imbalance in the mind, emotions, and body of the audience. They bring degeneration and disease and lead people toward anti-survival paths because they distort the equilibrium of the entire nature of the audience.

Authentic sacred dances are created to bring balance and to restore equilibrium between Spirit and matter, between the future and the present, between the individual and humanity, between man and God.

Dancing is a way to receive nourishment. If your dance is physical, you receive physical food. If your dance is emotional, your nourishment is made of astral energy. If you dance mentally, your nourishment is mental. If you dance spiritually, your food is spiritual. All four foods are necessary for your survival. An ideal dance provides these four foods equally from four domains and creates equilibrium in your receiving, assimilating, and expressing systems. This is what great dancers accomplish.

Of course to receive such food, you need the proper organs. To digest that food, you need the proper organs. To express and radiate the products of your assimilation, you need the proper mechanisms. The construction of all these mechanisms must proceed regularly and synchronously within all four realms.

A dancer is the result of agelong labor to prepare his nature to be able to dance to the music of life, to assimilate life and bring in the "life more abundant."

We assimilate food with our fourfold nature (physical, emotional, mental, and spiritual). Food provides all four elements, but we can only assimilate those elements for which we have a corresponding digestive system. If only our physical digestive system is in operation, we can take in physical nourishment, while all other parts of our nature remain hungry.

Dancing prepared on the fourfold basis and properly executed gradually opens higher and higher mechanisms of digestion. Any mechanism that is not nourished becomes food for those that are nourished. This is a very mysterious fact. When your mental body is not nourished, it becomes food for your astral body.

Temple dances create those conditions in your nature and those elements that assist you in digesting your food in a fourfold way. In sacred dancing, your habits are broken; your negative emotions are gone; your mental crystallizations are dispersed; your spiritual fire is kindled. Such a situation makes it impossible for your nature to be poisoned by irritation or hatred. Ideal conditions for the body to grow and unfold its innate beauty are accomplished by sacred dancing.

Some foods we eat are cursed; they contain elements of irritation from passing through the hands of so many people. Our food must be blessed before it is eaten to disperse the curse.

As a result of sacred dancing, your nature becomes so integrated that at the time of eating, you feel the nature of the food and determine whether you must eat it or not. Dancing creates sensitivity in your vehicles; your etheric, astral, mental, and psychic natures sense the condition of objects, people, and events and warn you if things are dangerous for you.

It is interesting to note that if one does not receive emotional food, he becomes physically fat. If he does not receive mental food, he becomes emotionally congested with many confusing forces. If he does not receive spiritual energy, everything in his mind crystallizes. Dancing clears such a situation; food is assimilated evenly by the entire nature. This is how one becomes a beautiful, harmonized human being.

The food of the bodies is not taken only from the physical food that we eat but also from food that is emotional, mental and spiritual. Emotional, mental, and spiritual foods each contain four elements that nourish the fourfold nature of man. Suppose you eat healthy mental food; you can also nourish your physical body, astral body, and spiritual nature from this food. If you eat pure spiritual food, you can also nourish the rest of your bodies with elements which are not otherwise available to your bodies.

Great Ones do not live on physical food but on the food of Spirit. Of course, Their digestive systems are perfected to assimilate spiritual food for Their specific needs. It is through dancing that various kinds of subtle foods are assimilated by the bodies. When the nature of a human being is healthy, each vehicle shares its food with the other.

Emotional food is composed of beauty, harmony, and rhythm. Mental food is mostly thoughts, light, visions, and plans. Spiritual food is enthusiasm, ideas, purpose, will energy, and so on. A time will come in the life of each human being when he will nourish his entire mechanism with spiritual food alone and assimilate it through sacred dancing.

Those who want to participate in sacred dancing must begin refining their emotions and minds, as well as their physical bodies, and come in contact with their spiritual nature. This will make them safe as they dance and expose themselves to higher voltages and energies, and as they express these through their fourfold nature.

Chapter 24

Preparation for Dance

To become prepared to learn sacred dancing, there are practical steps which can be taught only by personal contact. But enough can be given here to help begin the process.

Physical Preparation

1. Run two to three miles each day, or swim for one hour. Of course, one can begin by running a shorter distance and then increase.

2. Focus on body posture and graceful movements.

3. Engage in happy and joyful relationships with others.

4. Study meaningful books, appreciate art objects, religion, philosophy, or science.

5. Study beauty, harmony, and rhythm not only through observation, reading, and discussion but also through deep and continuous meditation and experimentation.

Emotional Preparation

Express positive emotions through movements, such as

- gratitude
- love
- compassion
- hope
- joy
- ecstasy
- harmony

Expression of movements involves facial expressions, eyes, gestures, and so on. A dancer must be able to continue these exercises until he can distinguish between those energies he is directing through his emotional body or his physical body. For example, he must feel specific sensations if he is transmitting gratitude, hope, or others.

The dancer must not only practice the expression of positive emotions during this particular period of exercise. He must also continue this process throughout the entire day, in all of his relationships.

Mental Preparation

This is a more advanced stage in which the dancer must begin to express thoughts, ideas, and visions through his body after charging them with his emotional force. The dancer must have a special period of time to practice these expressions, slowly dramatizing them through his movements. He must charge his movements not only with positive emotions but also with constructive and lofty thoughts, ideas, and visions.

For example, stand up and make conscious movements. Try to put lofty emotions, thoughts, and spiritual fire into each movement. To be successful at this may take months, even years, but such an exercise will help you like a vitamin, regenerating and charging your whole being.

The next step is to work to eliminate fear, anger, jealousy, vanity, and ego from your nature. Such emotions and crystallizations prevent or hinder the flow of energies from expressing, or they mix poison into the emotions, thoughts, and movements of the dancer, spreading that poison throughout your body and to the audience.

We build a "circuit of fear" in our mental body when we pass through intense fear for the first time. All elements involved in that event form parts of this circuit. Time passes and we forget the event. Other positive events cast a shadow over the initial circuit of fear. But the circuit remains within us in full power, subjectively controlling our relationships and activities whenever any element of

218 The Creative Sound Wait.

that circuit is stimulated. Additionally, we connect new wires to that circuit over the course of time as we pass through new forms or events of fear. Eventually we construct a network of sensitive wires that connects our physical, emotional, and mental bodies.

We feel the shock of this circuit whenever an event we read about in the newspaper, hear on the radio or television, receive through letters, conversations, or actual experiences connects our consciousness to that network, that circuit of fear. Some people continuously live in the "force field" of that circuit, as every minute they are stimulated by something in their environment or their memory. This field eventually paralyzes the activities of the person, causing various kinds of diseases in him or leading him into those activities which are antisocial. The circuit of fear leads a person into covert activities and makes him hateful, criminal, and destructive.

To make people healthy, happy, prosperous, and sane, our leaders in all departments of society must cooperate to eliminate various fear techniques that have been in use by people and authorities for so long. Fear can be replaced with education, joy, right human relations, and dedicated service. It can be eliminated by creating security for people. Leaders must plan how to protect the rights of all people and how to educate those who violate the rights of others.

The circuit of fear creates a sediment which enters the bloodstream and weakens the circulatory system. It specifically attacks the hemoglobin and paralyzes the white blood cells.

Most symptoms of deficiency are the result of living under the pressure of fear. When fear coalesces for years, the person loses his defense mechanism and becomes the prey of every kind of virus and germ.

It has been observed that fear destroys creativity and deters the flow of energy. Sacred dancers and creative artists must use any techniques available to them to prevent fear and to develop fearlessness.

The same thing applies to anger, jealousy, vanity, and ego. Such elements degenerate the entire dance mechanism built by the artist. The purer the artist, the greater will be his effect on the audience.

Another step is to learn how to meditate. Meditation opens the path of contact with higher spiritual configurations which form the basis of Temple or sacred dances. Meditation enables you to detach yourself gradually from your various mechanisms and experience your True Selfhood.

In meditation, a moment comes in which you observe how your mind operates. This is the stage in which true meditation begins. The observer is you; you are able to detach yourself from your mind, through which you were thinking. Now you withdraw yourself out of the mind into yourself; now you can think without using the mind. This is true meditation.

Generally, it is the mind that thinks, like a programmed computer. But the real Thinker is the human soul.

For a long time, the soul operates the computer, just as it is programmed. A time comes, however, when the human soul no longer operates the mental body but thinks, observes, and knows himself. This is called the stage of straight-knowledge, or direct knowledge, which is accomplished without using the reasoning or logical mind. This stage is one degree lower that Intuition.

Intuition is related to planetary, solar, and galactic relationships and knowledge. Straight-knowledge is related to the individual life, achieved through meditation.

Of course, meditation is a gradual ascent. One needs years of faithful practice. But remember, all efforts and labor are never lost; they prepare you for your future glory.

Great dancers are created from those who go through such a regimen of exercise for a long period of time. After following through with these disciplines, the manifestation of a perfect dance surges out of the dancer from the inner side of life.

Chapter 25

Practicing Movements

When you feel that you are able to express your higher nature through your movements, then it is the time to begin practicing them with a few other dancers, observing each other and helping each other express in better and deeper ways. The same thing must then be repeated in group formation.

The next step is to exercise communication through movements, without speech or words. Such a communication must slowly develop into a conversation through movement. After one hour of exercise, the participants must discuss whether they were understood through their movements.

Care must be taken not to remain on one level but to converse as emotions, as thoughts, even as spiritual ideas, incorporating all of these in the movements.

Always try to use your imagination if you are conversing emotionally; use visualization if it is mental; use telepathy if it is spiritual. Telepathy can also be used in mental conversation. Later, you will learn the science of impression to express your real spiritual ideas and higher visions. One must not forget that all of these elements must be expressed through appropriate movements.

Actually, humanity once knew this science but forgot about it. Animals use the language of movement and understand each other perfectly through it. Along with their movements, they also use their voice to express the deeper meanings of their movements.

You can work from an easy subject to a more complicated and abstract one. For example, you can converse about a flower, tree, river, or forest. Then try to express emotions, such as love and gratitude, and then move on to express simplicity, freedom, and joy. Eventually you may converse about Infinity, space, and immortality.

Dancing is an effort to manifest the beauty, mystery, and glory latent within us. It is not easy to manifest these. It takes hard, creative labor performed step by step and often repeated. Your dance can be the expression of natural beauty, of the joy of Nature, or it can demonstrate deeper psychological revelations, dreams, aspirations, and striving. It can demonstrate the mystery of the soul, a journey to other worlds, spatial configurations, and so on. It may also demonstrate the formation of virtues — their growth, blooming, and results.

I once saw a dance which demonstrated the growth and unfoldment of three flowers simultaneously. It was so magnificent that the whole audience cried in ecstasy. Temple dances were created to transform life and make our life a sacred dance played under the lights of the stars on the stage of Infinity.

A small group of dancers trained together can create a story and try to express the story through their movements, words, and music. There are shades of meaning and emotions which are impossible to express in words; sometimes only gestures and facial expressions can convey the meaning, while at other times only the voice can express it.

The following exercises are helpful in learning how to express yourself through movement. They should be practiced, putting more and more of your nature in them as you progress.

Exercise One

This exercise requires a minimum of five people. In this exercise, the participants are allowed only to move their arms, hands, and eyes. After learning how to do it properly, a slight movement in the spine may be introduced.

1. Breathe in deeply and exhale all that you can. Do this five times.

2. Relax a moment and visualize that your fourfold nature is integrating and aligning within your light — as a soul.

3. Put your right palm over your heart and give your heart energy to each other in a movement that conveys a giving form. Repeat this a few times until you really feel that you are giving your heart energy to each other.

4. In the meantime, try to focus your mind on your movements so that your mind does not waver to any other subject or object.

5. As you continue in this exercise, try to charge your movements with pure spiritual energy and joy. Do this for as many times as necessary, until you feel that you are actually passing your spiritual, mental, and emotional energy to each other and are taking care not to fall into mechanicalness.

If at any time you feel as if you are tired or are lacking focus, stop the exercise. Do not resume the exercise until you feel the urge from within yourself to do so.

Exercise Two

Close your eyes and visualize yourself going through all the movements of the above exercise. Repeat this seven times.

Exercise Three

Close your eyes and send your love to someone with movements of your arms, hands, head, and spine.

Exercise Four

Repeat Exercise Three, this time adding movements of your leg or legs.

Exercise Five

Open your eyes and move your eyes as gracefully as possible. The movements must be slow so that you have time to imagine, visualize, or even contemplate.

Exercise Six

Keep the image of the one you love in your mind, as if he or she were close to you.

Exercise Seven

1. Repeat Exercise One, this time moving your hands, arms, neck, head, spine, and legs — taking steps in harmony with your other movements.

2. Let the whole group try to make the same movements, as close to each other as possible. All movements must synchronize as if the group were one person, controlled by one soul.

3. Repeat this exercise daily until all movements are totally synchronized. This may take several months.

Exercise Eight

1. Try to send freedom to people to make them free, using the same methods as Exercises One through

Seven, but substituting the idea of freedom in your movements instead of the giving heart sending love.

2. Notice how and why the movements are different.

3. Imagine, visualize, and direct your energy to make people free. Start individually, then in group formation.

4. Work on synchronized movements until you feel that you have the energy of freedom in your being and you can send it to others through your dancing.

Exercise Nine

1. Try to create a dance to bless the entire world, incorporating the following:

   • Choose a place for the dance.

   • Remember the entire earth.

   • Remember many kinds of people.

   • Remember oceans, rivers, lakes, waterfalls.

   • Remember winds, tornadoes, earthquakes, fires.

   • Remember vegetation, animals, birds, fish.

2. Think about how and why you are going to bless the earth.

3. Prepare the music, the words, the colors, and movements.

4. Make this a group dance, using all of your creative imagination to make it so effective and influential that you feel you are bringing about certain changes in the world.

Exercise Ten

After dancing Exercise Nine, the "Dance of Blessings," try to dance the "Future of the Earth." Demonstrate the present. Then dance how things are changing through your movements and group configurations.

I saw a dance which took the energy of blessings from the Chalice in the head and formed a twelve-petaled Chalice with the dancers. Each petal of the Chalice spread blessings to all kingdoms of the earth, with different movements and configurations. The costumes of the dancers were black from the waist to the feet with a large yellow belt. Each dancer had a different colored shirt, symbolizing the twelve petals of the Chalice.

You can perform this dance differently. For example, you can symbolize the Chalice by using a cup or the space between the dancers in the circle and take the energy of blessings and distribute them to earth.

Exercise Eleven

This is an exercise which you can do to open the flow of energy from the inside to the outside.

1. Close your eyes and visualize a seed in your palm. Put the seed, with appropriate movements, into the earth. Bless it.

2. Using creative imagination, see how the seed emerges from the earth and becomes a bud of a flower, until slowly the whole beauty of the flower unfolds in front of your eyes.

Remember the colors, movements, and sounds you experience as you perform this exercise. Remember that you are not only imagining the process but also that you are demonstrating the whole process with your movements, music, and color.

The synchronized movements of a group charged with spiritual force is a source of a tremendous amount of psychic energy.

At first you may think that it is impossible, but eventually you are going to choreograph an entire dance, create the music, and through the use of proper costuming and scenery send higher energies to the audience. This becomes possible if you start with enthusiasm. Some groups use swords, sticks, or daggers as props while others perform using only their hands, feet, head, and body. You may choreograph the best dance ever seen in the world!

You can use your creative imagination. With your dance, show the opening of the petals of a flower, present a bird singing to the flower, or even show how the fragrance of the flower is spreading in the air. You can even be the seed, the process of growth, the breakthrough into the new world, the bud, the flower, the fragrance, and so on.

As you involve yourself in the process of creating a dance, go more deeply into your subject matter. Never begin a new dance without perfecting the previous one. By rereading this section occasionally, you will refresh your memory with how many ways one can use dancing.

Remember that you do not yet have a Teacher, and you are not performing for him. You are learning certain secrets of dance and preparing yourself to be sensitive, expressive, and creative for that time when the Teacher takes you into his hands.

What Dances Do

In urging yourself to translate abstract concepts through physical movements, voice, sound, music, and color, you open channels of expression for your Inner Glory, which slowly begins to manifest and activate. Through your creative efforts, you give new birth to yourself in another world.

When I first came to America, I was an officer in a church. I had a school attended by forty children who were so undisciplined and wild that I could not understand the reasons why. They used to do whatever they wanted to do in the classroom.

At first I showed them anger, used force and hard discipline, but it did not work. They became worse and their parents began to attack me. Eventually I decided to teach them to dance. I collected them and showed them how to walk, how to do certain exercises, and how to dance

Temple dances. Two weeks later, they were sweet, disciplined, and respectful children, eager to learn the dances. They used to come half an hour early to learn them.

Through the dances I taught them how to

- respect others
- express gratitude
- relate with their parents and other family members
- eat
- be clean
- be punctual
- study in class

The parents of these children were surprised by how much they had changed. Then I started teaching them simple movements to do with their parents. Many family problems were solved, and attendance at lecture time increased to seventy percent.

With these exercises I learned that through Temple dances, human beings create contact with their higher selves and become more solemn, disciplined, considerate, and striving, and they live a more purposeful life. Temple dances transform the lives of people.

Music is very important to the dance. The ascending and descending tones must control the movements. It is the music that must orchestrate the movements; perfect harmony must exist between the music and the movements. Movements are related to the octaves; as the notes rise or fall, the corresponding movement must rise or fall in the same rhythm, synchronizing with the speed of the music. Movements that do not synchronize with the music create disturbances in our mental and emotional realms, increasing pressure in our body. This is why dancers used to practice a long time to synchronize their walk and movements with the music and notes.

Some Hindu sacred dances are very advanced in synchronizing all the movements of the face, eyes, head, and body — even making various movements with different parts of the body in harmony with the entire piece of music. Hindu sacred dances are far more advanced than any dance found in the western world. One must be spiritually far advanced to perform such dances.

For healing dances, one must study human anatomy, learn the notes of every organ, and the type of energy controlling each specific organ. In creating a healing dance, the dancer generally uses three kinds of energy — light, love, and will power — according to the organ and the level of the person.

When all of this is understood, you transmit energy through your movements. Imagine how the energy reaches the target. Visualize the changes occurring in the organs in etheric matter. Your healing will be more effective if you visualize the etheric body and the etheric organs, rather than the physical body and the physical organs. Every change must be introduced into the physical body through the etheric body. Attention focused on the physical body often creates violent reactions.

In healing, different musical instruments can better tune themselves with different parts or organs of the body. One must try to discover the relationship between the instrument and human nature. Some music can fail to reach the target when played on the piano, while if it is played on the violin, it easily hits the target. The drum and its beat sets every chakra in our etheric body in its speed and general rhythm. The drummer must know what beat to use and in what rhythm and tonality.

If one is clairvoyant, he does not have any difficulty seeing the relationship between the beat of the drum and the centers. But one can discover such a relationship through long experimentation. Certain drum beats energize the stomach. If you use that beat while trying to heal the heart, you fail or further complicate the problem.

Some people know this science instinctively, and they are able to create the corresponding beat for every occasion.

It is also important to consider the power of the dancers. If one or five dancers cannot heal, perhaps fifteen to twenty dancers could heal, provided that they are all synchronized in all their vehicles and know how to assimilate and transmit energies.

In the future, when the art and the science of dancing is perfected, two hundred people could change the destiny of mankind and lead humanity toward a new transformation.

Let us now look at a few other exercises, that are a little more complicated than those previously given.

Exercise Twelve

1. Orchestrate a dance in which you have found a small wounded bird in the forest. Take the bird to your heart.

2. Go and share this joy with your friends. Experience their joy and let them express joy in their movements and motions.

3. Put the bird in a safe place. Watch over him all night. Then the next day, feed him and let him recover and fly away.

4. Dance your joy. Express gratitude that such an opportunity was given to you to save the bird.

5. Let your friends praise and honor you, and, together, dance a farewell dance to the bird.

Exercise Thirteen

1. You are sitting in your room when the telephone rings. A depressed friend is asking for your help; he is going to commit suicide.

2. Express your care and emotions in dance. Go see him; cheer him up with your dance, and make him dance with you and be charged with hope and joy for the future. All of this must be seen in your dance.

Exercise Fourteen

1. News arrives that a close friend of yours, whom you love dearly, has passed away.
2. Close the doors and windows. Then dance your sorrow.
3. Then incorporate the idea of immortality and closeness to him. Rejoice, and let your dance show this change. Open the windows and enjoy his presence, as if he were dancing with you as a spirit.

We find examples in Shakespearean literature and the works of other great writers throughout history of how one can draw the congested tension accumulated by tragedies in life and release them, freeing people in the audience who were under the pressure of such tragedies. There is a law of correspondence in the Universe. Something similar to what you have within yourself can draw it from others to the surface.

Geniuses knew this and they orchestrated dramas and tragedies to pull similar conditions out from within those who were watching. Such therapeutic methods were surpassed in Temple dances. Through dancing, not only is the congested and rotten event buried within the person loosened and brought to the surface, but it is also consumed and dissolved forever. This is done with the part of the dance which shows how you can master your problems in the vision of Immortality, Infinity, and Timelessness.

Dancing with colors, movements, and music brings down your fiery essence, which then consumes the wreckage of events drawn out from the inner corners of your subconscious. This is why Temple dances end with movements of hope, future, victory, and joy. The elements produced by hope, future, victory, and joy dissolve the infection that is drawn out of your system.

Notes on Exercises:

Every form created in your mind, every form existing in your mind has an effect upon your body, emotions, even upon your mind itself and upon your life and environment. This is why with every exercise one must observe the changes occurring in your nature and environment. It is wise not to hurry and not to be slow. If you are too fast, you create barriers on your path which you cannot overcome. Your own barriers defeat you. If you are too slow the speed of others creates extreme trouble for you. You must find the pace at which you want to progress and do your exercises accordingly.

It is possible that these exercises can create immediate and fantastic results, but for the long run they can be dangerous if hurried and forced. This is why we are told to "make haste slowly."

The suggestion is to do the chosen exercise once a month and watch the effects. Then you will be able to judge. Maybe twice or three times will be enough for one year.

Circular movements in dancing or in rhythmic walking create a mighty pool of energy. Rotating and going in the direction of the circle is more powerful. We see this in the movement of the earth and heavenly bodies. It is this movement that creates centrifugal fire, even an axis and an identity. Each axis is the condensation of energy gathered through rotating and revolving.

Certain Dervishes and Sufis knew this principle, but in general they dissipate their energy instead of condensing it around themselves. They are not on the wrong path, but their circular motions are not scientifically accurate and are not in harmony with the ratio of the movements of the earth and solar system.

Remember also that you have three bodies. Besides the physical, you have etheric, astral, and mental bodies. In dance and in movements the participation of these three bodies is imperative, or else you create chaos in your system and environment if all your three bodies are not engaged in the dance or movement. This means, in simple words, that you must be emotionally, mentally, and energetically involved in the dance or movement, as if you were the dance, not the dancer.

When your body dances and your imagination is somewhere else or if you are thinking about other objects of interest, you are not really dancing.

To dance means to attract, to accumulate, and to radiate energy. This is possible only when all your bodies are synchronized. When you watch people entering a room, you immediately feel if they are or are not carrying energy within themselves.

Those who are integrated, together, and synchronized when entering a public place make people feel their presence and respect them. Those who do not carry energy are overlooked and left alone.

The same thing applies to dances or ritualistic or ceremonial movements.

Chapter 26

Breaking Patterns

One of the rules of advancement and progress is that a person must break the patterns in which he is living and strive for something new. We must break those patterns which exist in our emotional, etheric, and physical bodies and build new patterns. If old patterns continue to exist in the etheric plane, in a person's nervous system and brain cells, echoing and re-echoing, they reinforce the old structure of his moral, spiritual, and physical make-up and he will never be able to progress. A breakthrough must be made.

When we listen to music and the voices of people around us, to the radio, television, and even to voices that we cannot hear, they affect us and build certain patterns in our etheric body. These patterns must be broken. New kinds of movement, thinking, and feeling and new kinds of music can create a new pattern in our physical, emotional, and mental realms.

That is why the unusual, special movements used in Temple dancing were created. The movements may look ordinary, but when they are combined with music and the right kind of thinking and visualization, a totally new combination results.

Temple dancing integrates the physical, emotional, and mental vehicles. When these three bodies are integrated by the use of music and dance movements, psychic energy starts to flow without creating any friction.

One of the reasons for sickness, weakness, and illness is that psychic energy accumulates or creates friction in our nature. This is a fact that new methods of medicine and psychology have not yet observed. When psychic energy accumulates somewhere in the emotional, etheric, or mental bodies, it creates friction unless there is proper circulation. Dance and movement, music and thinking, color and different symbolisms combined together create a flow in the system so that wherever there is congestion, it disappears, taking with it the effect it had on the physical body. When the congestion found in the etheric, emotional, or mental body is removed, the corresponding effect in the physical body disappears.

Temple dances were very sacred in India, Persia, Greece, and in the Aztec and Mayan cultures. Ancient civilizations had various dances, the purpose of which was to integrate the physical, emotional, and mental

vehicles. This process of integration then opened channels for the circulation of psychic energy, energy that is
coming from the Soul.

When we move our hands, feet, or head, something happens which is not generally observed. We touch
the etheric web of the planet, the electrical web of the
planet, with the electricity that is in our hands or other
parts of our body. For example, when you touch a door-
knob after walking across a carpet, what happens? A
shock occurs. Electricity exists in many levels, and when
a person moves, he puts that electricity into action.

When a person moves, he touches the etheric web
of the planet. Because we contain electricity, we create
a phenomenon in the etheric web of Nature equal to the
amount of the electricity we expend. If the electricity is
coming from the physical body, the result is physical —
but it can also be emotional, mental, or spiritual.

Electrical currents coming from higher levels cause
one to fuse with the etheric web of the planet, creating
far-reaching phenomena in the etheric web of the planet in
the form of color and sound. Color changes into sound at
one level; sound changes into color at another level. This
attracts the attention of inhabitants of these planes, like a
call, and certain phenomena are produced in response.

For example, what happens if you bait a hook and
throw it into the lake? A fish sees it and is attracted to it,
perhaps because of the waves, the color, the magnetism, or other factors. Similarly, when a person contacts the etheric web through his movement, he creates an

electrical phenomenon in the electrical field of Nature, the result of which is equal to the power that he puts behind his movement.

We cannot see the colors and sounds we produce in this manner because they are beyond the frequencies which we can physically perceive, beyond our vision and hearing. But this does not mean that they do not exist. A television set that is not properly tuned or only has a certain range cannot pick up or properly interpret the various programs that are being aired. But by adjusting the set properly, it can clearly project the pictures it is being sent — which is a process of magnetism, electricity, contact, and tuning in.

We are many times more sensitive than a television set. Whether we sit or stand, whatever we do, whatever movement we make creates a corresponding action and reaction in the etheric web of the planet. The Great Sage advises us not even to move our hand unless it is necessary. Whenever we move, we put energy into action.

It has been observed that people move and act according to their level of consciousness and beingness. Advanced people walk and speak differently than average people. There are people who can walk in the presence of the Great Ones; there are people who feel paralyzed in Their presence. This is all due to different phenomena of energy.

An advanced Initiate radiates high-level energies as he walks, putting into action high-level energy currents in space. His walking uplifts people and orients them toward higher aspiration. Whatever energy a person radiates into space, he evokes a similar energy from space.

Say, for example, that there is a fly on your head and you hate that fly, so with violent anger you try to chase it away. Through such an action, you radiate waves of *imperil*, or irritation, into space. Space reacts to your movements with similar force, which spreads disturbing effects in your environment and through your body.

Imagine how poisonous and destructive are the effects of criminal actions — physical, emotional, and mental actions. We must understand that thinking, feeling, emotional expression, and action all create a reaction or response from the electrical sphere of the world. We do not often care about what we do on such levels. But we are, and our life is, the result of what we do.

It is possible to charge our physical actions or movements with various thoughts and feelings, and enact them in various geometrical forms. Each of them will create different results. We can further charge our actions with our looks, voice, and facial expressions, and create different results. This explains how different kinds of dances affect a person's life, his future, and those who are in some way related to him.

A living being is a source of influence. One can influence people unconsciously or consciously. Any influence one makes upon others is what he gives to Nature; Nature will return in kind what is given to Her.

Temple dances are a way to influence people consciously for purposes of healing, uplifting, inspiring, and enlightening them. Temple dances not only receive certain reactions and responses from spatial energies and forces but also from the audience. If the dancers radiate high-level energies through their dancing, color, movement, and music, their higher natures respond to the dance in the form of greater enthusiasm. Thus, the whole atmosphere becomes electrified. Healing can occur in the audience as a result, and a healing wave also is sent into space from the place where the dance occurred.

An orchestra produces a higher-level performance if it has an inspired and enthusiastic conductor. The conductor, with his ability to interpret the music, charges the musicians with his inspiration and enthusiasm, which helps them play better and more powerfully influence the public. The conductor moves and directs the orchestra with his special movements. If the conductor has no enthusiasm or does not understand the spirit of the piece that is being played, the orchestra will have a shallow influence or even a negative influence on the audience.

Dance is the interpretation of music, of an idea, vision, feeling, thought, or emotion, expressed through movements which influence people in different ways. A specific movement, color, or sound is related to a corresponding center in the body. Combinations of movement, color, and sound affect the lower or higher centers in the dancers and the audience. They can even create different secretions of our glands. All secretions emanate different substances into the air which are absorbed by the audience.

Dance and movement are also like conversations — building sentences, paragraphs, and chapters. Certain dances do not say anything; some ramble on insanely; some movements are arranged in such a way that there is no link between any word or meaning; some are complete statements; some are not. A good dance or movement must resemble a good speech — full of meaning, reason and logic, feeling and interpretation, energy and vision. The spirit of the audience feels whether the "sentence" is complete or incomplete.

Thus, the effect of dance and movement on Nature and humanity depends on the degree of wholesomeness, health, and completeness of the dance — or its incompleteness and unhealthiness.

I knew a dancer who had a flowering shrub that was dying. She asked me one day if I knew something that would heal the plant, and as a joke I told her to dance for the shrub. A few months later when I visited her, the shrub was filled with exquisite blossoms. "How did you save the shrub?" I asked her. "Don't you remember telling me to dance for it?" she replied. I was more surprised than she. Later, she told me that she danced around the shrub a few minutes every day, playing music and singing — and it recovered.

In olden times, many different dances were performed for healing. This tradition still lives today in various parts of the world.

The consciousness of a group of dancers can be found on intuitional, mental, emotional, or physical levels. A group of dancers can distribute energies to an audience more efficiently if it is a multidimensional group because it can reach every kind of person in the audience. Because each dancer shares all that exists in the group, each individual's influence not only comes from his own particular energy but also from the energy of the other members of the group as well.

For example, if a dancer is on the emotional plane, but dances with a multidimensional dance group, he not only radiates emotional energy to those who are emotionally receptive, but he also mixes the emotional energy with the other energies available and transmits them to emotionally-receptive people. Thus he helps them develop receptivity to higher kinds of energies. This is how a dance group can uplift the audience and help it make certain breakthroughs.

A dance group with a high level of radioactivity acts to transmit high-level spatial energies to earth. Dances performed by such a group can invigorate the planetary life. New energies from higher spheres help creative people, scientists, and leaders in their efforts to help humanity.

While watching a dance, the audience sees only the movements of the dancers' bodies. Remember, however, that with physical movements we also have movements of the mind, emotions, and energy. Sometimes a dance is made up of only one form of movement by part of the body, which does not correspond to movements made by the other parts. This creates a disturbance in the aura of the audience because the energy currents are not harmonious. Such a dance may appear harmonious from the outside, but the energies channeled through the dance are very disturbing. This disturbing influence creates various physical and psychological troubles in the dancers and in the audience. One of my dance Teachers used to tell us, "If you are not together within yourself, or if you cannot hold yourself together at least during the dance, please do not participate in the dance."

Temple dances must be scientifically and esoterically engineered and orchestrated. In the future, the mysteries of the Temples will be restored under the influence of great geniuses who will teach special people how to arrange initiation ceremonies — dance and movement, color, music, and fragrance — to fulfill the purpose of their rituals, ceremonies, and dances.

There is a tradition that says that Jesus danced with His disciples at various times. What kinds of movements did they make? What was their song, chant, or music? How coordinated and harmonized they must have been! What kind of energies did they transmit to the planet? How did they affect the lives of millions? What fires did they kindle that burn brightly, even to this day?

Tradition says that before the crucifixion, Jesus danced with His disciples.[1] This was a planned event because He and His disciples needed so much courage and strength to endure the suffering of the crucifixion and its consequences. Through the dance, they brought a tremendous amount of energy that kept the disciples together after Jesus left them, and urged them to stand on their own feet and continue spreading the Teaching of their Master.

Latin and Orthodox churches continue the tradition of such sacred dances through their beautiful rituals and ceremonies. By observing certain ceremonies, one can see how the entire congregation is in a slow-moving dance. For example, as the priest and his deacons walk through the congregation singing and with candles in their hands, the priest blesses with his cross while the deacons, with rhythmic movements, spread fragrance with censers. Others, dressed in beautiful vestments, sing while they carry symbols and pictures of the Lord. A sensitive person feels great upliftment in attending such ceremonies and rituals.

It is through such ceremonies and rituals that the energy of the Teaching of Jesus has been perpetuated for so many centuries. These ceremonies and rituals generally fulfilled the moral and spiritual needs of the multitudes for many centuries.

Armenian, Latin, Russian, and Greek churches and their affiliates work through energies more than through

1. See *Christ, The Avatar of Sacrificial Love*, pp. 123-135.

words and sermons. These churches transmit Christ-energy, instead of emphasizing sermons that are built by the power of the mental process. Intuition, feeling, energy, aspiration, and devotion are transforming and transmitting agents in their ceremonies and rituals.

In some Armenian and Latin churches, the congregation does not understand the language, but through the ceremonies and rituals, readings and hymns, transformation occurs in the congregation because of the energies that are invoked and evoked through the ceremonies — the slow, sacred dances.

Spiritual development is not based on any mental thoughtform or knowledge but upon the assimilation of energies. The Holy Spirit is not evoked by sermons, learning, and discussions but by devotion, dedication, purity, aspiration, and spiritual striving. These are gifts that are received as a person harmoniously coordinates his entire being into a sacred dance.

Dances, rituals, and ceremonies speak to the heart. It is the heart which charges an individual, a group, or a nation. When evoked energies touch the heart, transformation begins.

The destruction of an individual or nation originates from degenerated dancing. This is a historical fact. When the dance practices of a nation become vulgar, stimulating the lower centers or creating disturbances within the centers, that nation slowly enters a period of widespread crime. People from the highest to the lowest office fall into various criminal practices — drug use, alcoholism, sexual license, stealing, killing, raping, and so on. Dishonesty becomes a widespread disease throughout the nation.

If one observes our current world situation, he will see that the greatest controlling agent for degeneration exists in vulgar, chaotic dance, music, and color. These affect not only the health of a nation but also its morality, strength, and economy.

Emanations that come from distorted music and dance create widespread degeneration in the electrical web of the planet and in the auras of people — with deplorable results. The planet and solar system have their own rhythms and chords. Great musicians can intuitively contact them and compose music, or orchestrate dances that are in harmony with the existing rhythms and chords.

Music and dance created by those who are involved in negative emotions, drugs, alcohol, feelings of revenge, or exploitation are not in harmony with planetary and solar rhythms and chords. What they create disturbs the network of energies, just as an out-of-tune instrument affects the whole orchestra.

It is not an expression of superstition to say that natural calamities occur because of distorted music and dance, distorted emotions, thoughts, and activities.[2] We must remember that we are part of the planetary and solar space. We "live, move and have our being" in space. Any agitation created in space through distorted dancing and music will naturally create drastic consequences.

---

2. See also, *Earthquakes and Disasters, What the Ageless Wisdom Tells Us.*

Music and dance are languages. If a person speaks nonsense all day long, or uses words and sentences without meaning, his mind will eventually degenerate. The mind is programmed for meaning; it is built like a calculator. If it is misused or damaged, it does not calculate properly. It is here to serve a specific purpose. It is created for Good. We are in the same relation to the planetary and solar Minds as words and sentences are to our mind.

Dance and music were originally offered as gifts to humanity. They were created to advance the evolution of humanity, linking the human body, emotions, and mind to higher rhythms, to higher ideas, visions, feelings, and geometrical formations. They were an effort to integrate humanity and align its consciousness with the consciousness of the planetary life and solar system.

Movement, dance, and music are given on a gradient scale. First they are given for the body; then for the body and emotions; then for the body, emotions, and mind. Finally they are given for the spirit in the form of sacred dances which nourish the spirit and include all the others. Sacred dances change according to their purpose, to the Rays of the location, to the level of evolution, and to the cycles of energy release.

We must remember that hand movements are especially instrumental in distributing energy from various centers or charging various centers. One must observe the results of movement, dance, and music upon the performers and the audience to learn of its effects. A dance teacher must be clairvoyant, or have a clairvoyant person assisting him, to see the effects of movement, dance, and music upon the performers and audience.

There are certain movements which resemble the actions of a monkey cooking dinner. He mixes sugar, pepper, and salt with water, then adds oil, vinegar, grain, nuts, and so on, trying to prepare the dish. Some movements are exactly the same way. They mix the energies of various centers, blocking some, opening others, imposing higher energies on lower centers and lower energies on higher centers, thus creating chaos in the individual. Such a condition eventually can be healed through performing intuitively and scientifically prepared movements, dance, and music.

We must remember that dance and music are the result of movements — movements of thoughts, emotions, speech, hands, eyes, face, gestures, and so on. Knowing this, we can say that a lecturer is also a kind of dancer. He is either graceful, coordinated, and rhythmic or he is chaotic.

Observe people when they are talking. See how much gracefulness they have; how their thoughts, feelings, and expressions harmonize and build a mysterious combination which we call gracefulness.

I once attended a lecture given by a woman whose speech was superb as far as her ideas and analysis were concerned. Additionally, her rhythmic hand movements, facial expressions, and manner of dress, hair style, and make-up all composed a total symphony for the audience.

When her lecture was over, I commented to her, "Your performance in its totality was a supreme dance." She gave me a graceful smile. If we can learn to be graceful, our entire life will gradually turn into a sacred dance.

On another occasion, I attended a lecture given by a young woman who was dressed in boots and a military-style dress. In a very masculine voice, she spoke of the importance of being tender, soft, and feminine at home, as well as in the business environment!

Dance, movement, music, and color will be used in the future to strengthen people, heal and enlighten them, and even create new senses in them. We read in history how kings used to have special dances performed to disperse their worries, to create energy and courage in them, to heal them and create sexual potency in them, or to release them from mental and emotional prisons. A cycle will come when specialized dance groups will perform a service for humanity.

One of the supreme goals of sacred dancing is to expand the individual's consciousness and create group consciousness in him. Sacred dance, music, and intuitively controlled movements release a person from crystallized patterns of energy, giving him freedom to expand and become more inclusive.

Sacred dances are instrumental in regulating us into the rhythm of Creation. It is through sacred dances that mankind will be able to expand its contact with the Cosmic Presence.

Chapter 27

The Origin of Temple Dances

The tradition says that when the Great Ones came to this planet 18,000,000 years ago, They saw that the humanity on earth was very slow in its evolution. Their minds were very primitive, they had very violent emotions, and they had huge bodies that were often uncoordinated in their movements.

The Great Ones thought that the best help would be to present music, movements, and dances to open their minds, refine their emotions, create integration in their bodies, and synthesize the whole human being.

So the Great Ones created musical instruments, and with rhythm and melody They taught human beings how to walk, how to do movements, and how to dance with the rhythm.

The tradition says that this method was very successful, and in forty to fifty years time They saw great changes in primitive man. Some of them were even able to sound a few notes and try to sing. The dances began as very simple movements, but gradually they became more complicated.

During this period, which was two to three hundred years, the Great Ones noticed that primitive man showed, to some degree, coordination. They began to use their arms, legs, fingers, neck, body, eyes, and to hear better and sound the notes more clearly.

Those who graduated from certain dances eventually were invited to the private halls to learn more complicated dances.

It is from these dances that eventually the dancers of the inner Temples were chosen for special performances.

Along with the dances They taught primitive arithmetic, geometry, and anatomy.

Of course the first goal of the Temple dances was physical coordination. Then they presented or created dances that were related to emotional refinement and coordination, then mental integration and refinement. Then eventually they were trained to heal, to uplift, and to guide and educate people with their dances, music, singing, and stories.

In the inner Temple, the dancing continued to transmit energies from constellations and stars and to direct these energies to groups, specific locations, and institutions.

In more advanced classes, the Masters taught how to use Temple dances to communicate with one's own Soul and with higher and creative forces in the Universe.

A moment came when the Masters retreated for certain reasons, and Their disciples and aspirants continued Their work. Here and there, certain individuals began to use the dances for the gratification of sex, war, and killing and created totally opposing dances, dances for lower pleasures or animalistic dances.

Primitive man's life, for a long period of time, was all dancing and singing. He never did anything without dancing and singing. For him, life was dance and song from sunrise to sunset. He worshipped in dancing and singing; he ate, walked, and made love in singing and dancing. He even killed animals and ate them as part of his dance. Killing enemies was also a dance and song.

Then the dance and song gradually went in the opposite direction. Those on the right path used it for the purpose it was given to them. The dark ones used it to turn the wheel of evolution backward.

What we see now in the field of dance and music is the growing seed of an ancient civilization. We have the same divisions. There are Temple dances taught under secrecy and after years of training; there are folk dances that are innocent in nature; and there are also dances prevalent in all nations that perpetuate the animalistic nature in man and block the path of his evolution.

In Temple dances They taught the mystery of rhythm, the effect of drums on the etheric and higher centers, the

258 *The Creative Sound*

science of transmission of energy, and the mystery of the manifestation of Divinity. They taught how the divine nature of man could awaken and eventually take incarnation and manifest as a leader or as a hero.

They taught how it was possible with rhythmic movements and chants to influence Nature to bring rain, sunshine, or clouds.

In the more secret Temples, They taught how to move mountains or walls through dances and chanting.

There were also dances that were performed to release the human soul during the process of death and lead him into the higher spheres.

Gradually dances and music were used in the ceremonies and rituals and in the mysteries of initiations.

It was revealed through the Temple dances that certain angelic hosts are related to movements, sound, music, and color. Through right movements, colors, and sound, those angelic forces were brought near humanity to assist in its evolution.

The ancients thought that space could be polluted with destructive thoughts, negative emotions, and criminal activities and that the polluted space could create famine, earthquakes, natural catastrophes, epidemics, etc. They thought that space could be cleared and purified only by dances and special music performed by those who had a pure heart and a pure life.

They also believed that the weather, abundance or famine, flood and fire were related to the pollution of space. The pollution in space disturbs the balance and equilibrium between the earth and space, causing all those phenomena that bring disaster to all living beings. The cure was dance and music, purposely created to restore balance and harmony and to purify space.

Disturbances in space are caused by those who have disturbances in their mind, emotions, and life.

In trying to restore the harmony in space, people do have a role to play in affecting the human life and gradually eliminating disturbances going on all over the world in the inner fields of man. Thus, real dance and music are agents of healing, restoring, and harmonizing.

Temple dances build a bridge between your personality and the Soul, if there is right intention behind your dancing.

It is important to know that dancers on the dark path cannot build this bridge, first, because the Solar Angel does not agree with them, if they have Solar Angels, and second, the human soul, or ego in the personality, cannot detach himself from the bodies and aspire to freedom.

When the dances are performed to speed the evolution of the human soul and offer a service for others, the human soul affects the physical, emotional, and mental bodies and gradually subjects them to his will through the rhythm and music. Then, instead of being captivated in the bodies, he disciplines them to do his will. Gradually the personality vehicles become more and more sensitive to the human soul, and they absorb his light and fuse with him.

It is after a certain degree of discipline that the human soul attracts the attention of the Solar Angel, and gradually the influence of the Solar Angel penetrates into the personality vehicles and helps the human soul to proceed further on the path of his freedom and fusion with It.

This is all done through the Temple dances, through the rhythm of movements, and through the rhythm of music and singing or chanting.

Thus, Temple dances are daily rituals to accomplish fusion with the human soul or personality vehicles and fusion between the human soul and the Solar Angel. Thus the dance is a daily ritual to accomplish the building of the bridge between the Higher Worlds and draw inspiration, ideas, visions and impressions for the service of all living forms in the Universe.

During the process of this ritual or dancing, the vision of the Soul slowly penetrates into the mental body, into the emotional and physical bodies, and brings them under the rhythm of Its vision. Thus the body, emotions, and thoughts align themselves to be a transmitter for the vision of the Soul.

Thus the dance and music not only coordinate your personality vehicles but also align them with your Soul, and it is through a coordinated personality and Soul that the Higher Forces can find an opportunity to reach humanity.

A group of people integrated in their personality and with their Soul can turn into a transmitter for the Hierarchical assistance to the world.

World affairs are conducted without higher assistance. That is the reason why we have so much suffering, pain, and waste.

All healing processes on the mental, emotional, and physical planes are the result of such integration, alignment, and coordination. The harmony and rhythm of the Higher Worlds may descend on earth if we create conditions for them.

You must have a daily ritual of dancing, coordinating yourself through music and rhythm, aligning yourself with your highest aspirations and visions, and charging yourself with higher influences to carry them to your environment — instead of spreading your negative moods, depressions, and antagonistic attitudes.

It is often possible that through your meditations, aspirations, and study you accumulate lots of energy and create congestion within your system. This congestion may create problems in your mental, emotional, and etheric-physical mechanisms. You must let this congestion dissipate by using these energies through rhythmic dance, rendered as a service for humanity.

One of my friends used to say, "Let us dance for the service of humanity and release energies of light, love, and beauty."

Through the rhythmic dance you bring a great amount of energy into your system, and if you are an advanced disciple, you can use it for others to lead them, to uplift them, to purify them, to enlighten them, or to stop them from certain undesirable activities.

You can change and transform the audience through your dance. Through your rhythmic dance you transmit to your audience the energy you accumulated in your system, or are accumulating in your system, during the dance. This energy is easily absorbed by the aura of the audience, causing in it purification, upliftment, and harmony. If the transmitted energy is of the highest quality, it may create higher aspirations in the audience and expand their consciousness.

Most people go to colleges or universities and accumulate knowledge to such a degree that in the rooms of their consciousness they become congested.

Congestions create resistance to knowledge, and resistance makes them misuse their accumulated knowledge or use it to gratify their lower pleasures. If such people engage themselves in a five minute daily ritual of Temple dancing, they will see an amazing change in their nature.

First, through the rhythm of music and dance, the furniture of knowledge accumulated in their minds will be coordinated and changed into units of energy.

Second, they will see a new vision in their life, a new aspiration in their heart, and courageously face their life to make it a path of achievement.

Third, dances will expand their consciousness to such a degree that they will be able to use all their information in constructive ways.

Q&A

Question: *Does the explosion of certain galaxies or stars create disturbances in space?*

ANSWER: Of course, yes. They create huge tidal waves in space. These reach every corner of existence, carrying with them certain substances, chemicals, and pressures and affecting all kingdoms, especially the human kingdom, through its cells and organs.

Certain explosions even create epidemics because of their electrical frequencies and chemistry. Others create massive depression, revolutions, and wars.

Almost all the wars are mobilized under the pressure of such explosions in space, or even on earth.

Question: *Is it possible to escape from such effects?*

ANSWER: Of course, if we begin to live a life of joy, love, beauty, sacrificial service, forgiveness, and mutual gratitude. Such virtues elevate the level of our consciousness to such a degree that these tidal waves of explosions no longer create reactions from our nature.

The best way to avoid a gale is to raise yourself above its level.

If the gale is blowing five thousand feet above the ground, a safe level to exist will be six thousand feet above the ground.

Dances and rhythmic music also create a certain shield that protects you from the stormy waves coming from space.

Wherever you perform Temple dances, you cause purification there. That is why you feel energy and purity in a place where people danced and sang or played music dedicated to the Higher Worlds or used for the liberation of humanity.

Dance and music and singing gradually give birth to your innermost Self.

Question: *Do you think that man is good in his essence?*

ANSWER: There is no doubt about it. All our religions, constitutions, and laws are established on the foundation of the essential goodness of man.

Man is a source of treasures. All progress of culture and civilization, all the beauty that the human being gave to the world are extensions of his essential glory, his essential goodness.

Evil, ugliness, and crime do not exist in the Core of man. They are pollutions on the surface accumulated during the ignorance of the human being. They are transient. The permanent One is the goodness — the inner reality.

All higher wisdom is founded upon the rock of the essential goodness of man.

Question: *You emphasized sound and color, but not motions only. Why?*

ANSWER: The origin of sound and color is motion. Without motion, you do not have sound and color. They are like a trinity. They always exist together. Motion in dance synthesizes the colors and sounds used in the dances, amplifies them, and makes them more influential.

> **Question:** *You said we can create Temple dances at home. How will we know that we are choosing the right music, color, and movements?*

ANSWER: First of all, let me explain that certain dances are called Temple dances for the simple reason that such dances help to unfold your essence and increase your spirituality, beauty, joy, freedom, expand your consciousness, and put you in contact with Higher Worlds.

I am assuming that this is the labor to which every Temple activity is dedicated.

Choosing the right movements, color, and music depends on your motive and vision. If your motive is high, universal, and inclusive, if your vision goes beyond your personal pleasures, arrogance, and ego and aims to contact the highest within you, you will evoke the assistance of your Soul in choosing the right movements, music, and color. Also, you can slowly improve all these three, by watching the "fruits" of your dance.

If you are more joyful, full of hope, freedom, aspiration, energy; if you feel healthier and can handle your relationships with other people more efficiently and selflessly, it means your choice of music, color, and movements is right.

But if the "fruits" are irritation, fatigue, sexual excitement, or anger, you are wrong in your choice, which means you do not have lofty motives, ideals, and visions.

It is your target that controls the movement of your bows and arrows.

As there are out of key notes, there are also out of key colors and motions. You gradually learn all these things during the dances, and eventually, by your experiments and experience, you learn to do your best.

Do not forget that your aim in dancing is to translate your inner vision, inner ideal, inner goal through motion, sound, and color and eventually create a form which can be played back again and again, producing the desirable results. The more you dance, the more you discover finer points and can introduce changes to make your dance an ideal means for the desired ends.

Motions and colors or sounds can also be highly disturbing, but as you continue, you filter them and create better motions, better colors, and more goal fitting music.

The Great Ones were far advanced in the science of motion, color, music, and rhythm, and as a chemist uses the elements scientifically to prepare some formulas, the Great Ones used sound, motion, rhythm, and color to create the formula to promote human transformation and perfection.

In Temple dances, the Teachers are very careful to chose the dancers from those who have not only beautiful bodies but also healthy bodies. Any unhealthy condition in the body changes the energy currents and makes it destructive, or at least ineffective.

This is also true for the health of the emotional body. If the emotional body is infected by hatred, anger, fear, jealousy, revenge, malice, or treason, the incoming energies not only damage the dancer but also transmit toxins to the audience.

Also, if the mental body is sick with vanity, ego, separatism, greed, or illusions, the incoming energies change into destructive energies, even if the dance is presented as it was planned.

This is why the Temple dances slowly vanished from the public and were replaced by dances that have no spiritual aim but the pleasure of the body.

Some Teachers, during the choice of a dancer, immediately notice all kinds of defective points in the candidate as he walks. Walking clearly indicates if you have certain weaknesses or problems in your personality vehicles — to the eyes of those who see through you.

Some Temple dancers are selected from their childhood and cared for over a long time until they are ready for the ritual of sacred dance. There were families in Asia who were known as the producers of the best dancers. Their children were selected, because of their health, joy, and beauty, to be educated for the sacred dances.

The Teachers not only teach the movements of dance, but also They instruct you in how to walk, how to sit, how to move your hands, your fingers, your legs, and your facial muscles while you are in your ordinary environment. They say that every motion transmits either a constructive or a destructive energy, and this is true as well of voice and conversations.

Temple dancers are the most coordinated human beings who bring us the fire of beauty and inspiration for glorious living.

Chapter 28

Temple Dances and Patterns

There are patterns in our aura.[1] Every time you think, every time you talk or act in the same way, every time you walk in the same way, you build a pattern in your aura. This is because, with all that you do mentally, emotionally, and physically, you bring into action certain forces in your aura. And when these forces flow in the same way for a long time, they create certain patterns in the mental, emotional, and etheric substances. Any energy or force directed to these patterns makes them control your mental, emotional, and physical actions as if they were programmed apparatuses.

When you have many patterns in your aura that are not in harmonious synchronization with each other,

---

1. See also *Aura, Shield of Protection & Glory.*

gradually the tension increases and conflict starts between them. They spend your energy; they sap it and make you weak. Also, they do not let you fit yourself to new conditions, handle new decisions, and have new responses and reactions because these patterns condition your outlook, conclusions, decisions, and translation of events.

At certain times — as Nature does — you must go through a process of destruction and cleansing so that you free yourself from the conditioning force of patterns and start to think, speak, and act independently in response to the new light and new conditions.

Many thoughtforms, feeling habits, and physical habits must go if we want to live a life of freedom, in harmony with the demands of the progressing life. Sometimes crystallized patterns in our aura resemble outdated machines that we use to solve our modern, complicated problems. This ends in great failure. Old ways of solving problems not only do not help us but also create unending problems with heavy consequences. This is why periodically we must clean our home — our mental, emotional, and physical rooms — and throw away all that cannot be used.

Of course, this is not an easy task. However, human nature and Nature as a whole go through such processes periodically in times of crisis. When crystallizations reach a saturation point, we slowly lose faith in the way we think, speak, feel, and act. But after such a feeling we still continue to live through our old patterns until we face a catastrophe.

It is not easy to see that we have trapped ourselves in our own patterns. People who have less crystallized patterns can help us to see this fact. Once we see, the battle starts between the old patterns and the new ones we are trying to construct.

These patterns can be better understood if you sit in a pool of colorful water or in a pool of mud and make certain movements with your hands. You can develop a whole new science of observing the formation of the patterns. The thicker your aura, the more lasting your patterns.

Certain movements create more complicated patterns; others are simple. But all of them are formed in your aura as you think, speak, feel, and act.

We must learn to realize that we create certain patterns in our aura as we think, speak, feel, and act. Many such patterns are destructive; many constructive. Many patterns create disturbances in our aura; many others create harmony in it. Once this is realized, then people will be cautious about what they think, say, and do.

One can imagine what the mental movements of malice and hatred do to the pool of the aura; what lying and slander do to the astral aura; what crime and theft do for the etheric aura. One must firmly realize that thought is action, emotion is action, and any deed done by the physical body is an action.

These crystallized patterns can be slowly dissolved if one consciously controls his mental, emotional, and physical actions and replaces his old patterns with new, more fluidic patterns. There is a whole science of movements that teaches how to dissolve these patterns on mental, emotional, and etheric levels through movements charged by emotion and thought. Through a physical motion, you can change the patterns of your emotional and mental aura, if that motion is charged with emotion and concentrated thought. This is the foundation of Temple dances, or the foundation of esoteric movements.

There are also so-called spiritual patterns that must be replaced by higher patterns through striving and enthusiasm. Spiritual patterns come into being when virtues or ideas do not grow and expand. They became goals instead of means. When the definition of spiritual principles is understood as the last limit of our penetration and understanding, they crystallize and eventually turn into hindrances when the human soul tries to outgrow his former limits.

Breaking the patterns in our aura helps to break the patterns in the world, just as, for example, changing your patterns in the mud pool changes the patterns of others to a certain degree.

Space is static energy. Energy is in motion only when there is form and action. Form creates polarity and flow of energy. Action uses the energy to create patterns. To create new energy flow in our aura, we must follow the same procedure. We must create a new form through a *new action*. This pattern can be created only through a unified action of spiritual, mental, emotional, and etheric forces. Unless they are present in full measure in every movement or action, no new pattern can be created and no change occurs in our nature.

Synchronization of these four elements is essential for new flows of energy. The intensity of the patterns in our aura depends on the ratio of the mixture of elements put in it during our experiences. For example, if you hurt your hand without having an emotional reaction or mental reaction — imagination, worries, and so on — you have a pattern in your etheric aura, but this pattern is not extended into the astral and mental auras. Of course, this is very rare, but it happens.

But if you have an accident that is heavily charged by imagination and thoughts of future problems, the pattern extends into the astral and mental realms and becomes a steady formation in your aura that conditions your thoughts, emotions, and actions to a greater or lesser degree.

Changing the patterns must be done with the same procedure. Our actions or movements must carry intense emotion, concentrated thought, enthusiasm, and striving. Sometimes etheric, astral, and mental energies cannot fight with old patterns. But when enthusiasm and striving are put in it, they effectively destroy the old patterns. Enthusiasm and striving bring in a new form of fiery energy from higher realms.

This is, in general, a basic formula for dance. Dance and movements change the patterns and let in a new circulation of energies, breaking off the old patterns that had prevented the movement of energy. This is true for mental, emotional, and etheric vehicles. Each vehicle has many crystallized patterns that must be destroyed so that new ones can be built. This must proceed progressively. Temple dances are composed by those who can see these crystallized patterns and create movements that can eradicate them.

On the mental plane our conversations build patterns. For example, in the old age we would say, "I belong to a special religion." The new era man will say, "I belong to all religions." An old age man would say, "I belong to my nation." A new era man will say, "I belong to all nations, to the solar system, to the galaxy ...to Cosmos." In the new era, a piece of space will not be labeled and separated as me, you, mine, and yours; but it will be dealt with and regarded as part of a whole.

The state of our consciousness produces the patterns of our thoughts, speech, habits of feeling, and actions. To change the chain of these patterns, we must change our consciousness and focus our new consciousness in our new thoughts, feelings, and actions.

Dance is an orchestrated movement to provide an opportunity for our thoughts and emotions to create a new pattern. Sometimes we wonder if really a new pattern does exist. It does not. A new pattern is one that makes the energy flow without creating congestions, habits, or crystallizations and that makes it circulate throughout our physical, etheric, emotional, and mental realms.

Any event of our life in which we are involved physically, emotionally, and mentally creates a sticky image in our aura. Although this image is in the state of a microfilm, it still affects our decisions, health, and thinking. A scientifically organized, threefold (mental, emotional, physical) dance can gradually destroy such accumulations and give man back his freedom. For such movements, one must use motion, emotion, thought, and visualization. These are all parts of the movement.

The movements must be concentrated where the congestion or accumulation of the events are, such as the

— sexual area

— stomach area

— heart-chest area

— throat area

— head area

These are the five locations in which most of the accumulations are. The movements of the feet, spine, shoulders, hands, and head must be integrated with knowledge to dispel the accumulations. In this process, music is a powerful factor, and especially the voice of the dancer.

But beyond all these comes the power of thought and visualization.

People do not conduct their lives in independence. It is the patterns that control them, giving them the illusion that they are the masters of their lives.

The dangers of your patterns increase in proportion to your advancement and position. A soldier will not be so dangerous with his patterns, but a president will be extremely dangerous when he acts under the power of his patterns. This means that all advanced leaders and officers of a nation must periodically go through sacred dances.

Old patterns prevent you from responding to the demands of the new era and make you act as if you were one thousand years behind. This is why most of our decisions are not constructive, nor do they fit into the demands of the new era.

This is also why history repeats itself and people cannot free themselves from the similar events even if they change parties or presidents. Creating new laws does not mean that we have created a new life. On the contrary, the creation of new laws is proof that old patterns are becoming violent and they must be inhibited by force!

Human history in itself is a great pattern in which the world is caught. With all our scientific education and economic advancement, we are now ready to annihilate the life of the planet. We are caught in the patterns of solving our problems by force, by war, by revolution, by crime, reinforced by the patterns of hatred, fear, revenge, and anger.

There are even people who try to perpetuate such patterns for their own material interests. But eventually they pay more than those who tried to eliminate such patterns. Fanaticism is the accumulation of certain patterns that do not let you see other values or expand your consciousness with the light of others. Such a pattern eventually brings your life into a great danger because it separates you from others and draws their antagonism toward you.

Inclusiveness leads to expansion. Fanaticism leads to isolationism.

People may think that if there is no pattern in their aura, then there is confusion. On the contrary, auric energies flow in certain divine patterns reflecting the patterns of the circulation of energy of the planet or solar system. These patterns relate you to global and solar interests if you do not superimpose upon them the patterns of your glamors, illusions, and formed habits.

The undesirable patterns are those which prevent the divine patterns from acting as bridges between man and the Higher Worlds. The divine patterns can be blocked by criminal acts, negative and destructive emotions, and selfish interests formulated by the mind. These divine patterns are strengthened by joy, beauty, freedom, goodness, justice, gratitude, and the thoughts dedicated to sacrificial service.

Dance is the process in which higher thoughts and higher emotions become creatively active and express themselves through movements patterned upon the original, natural patterns of the aura.

People may not believe that our thoughts, emotions, and actions reduce themselves into micro-patterns in our aura that become either harmonious or antagonistic to the original patterns. Crystallization in the aura occurs when imposed patterns of energy block the flow of the energy circulation of the natural patterns.

Dance and movement can be formulated upon natural patterns or upon imposed patterns. If a movement or dance is the expression of artificial, imposed patterns, then man crystallizes his aura more and more until he no longer has any opportunity to expand and grow. Such a crystallization blocks the relationship of natural patterns with the pure global and solar patterns. The interruption of relationship makes man lose his sense of direction. The sense of direction assists man to follow the energy threads leading to the Central Magnet in the Cosmos.

Low order patterns can contaminate the auras of other people, impressing them with similar patterns. In olden days, the aura was spoken of as being a seamless cloth or robe. Its purity must be kept immaculate. This is why as one advances he tries to keep away from people and locations where many negative, anti-survival, and destructive patterns exist.

Infection of patterns also occurs through sexual relations. When such patterns are transmitted to the next person, they grow in size and strength and form the basis of strong glamors and illusions.

Patterns in your aura do other things. For example, they make you forget things. This is a very special fact for consideration. Patterns intercept the continuity or associative relationship of the other patterns, and you do not register in your brain a certain continuity. This is why we forget things. As old age settles in, we have manifold collections of patterns, and these patterns slow down our thinking and feeling, and even harden the arteries and nerve channels.

Detachment from such patterns is very difficult. This worldly life is a continuous and forceful attachment to various states of consciousness, feeling, and behavior. Attachment is a process of superimposition of artificial patterns on your aura. Our whole religious, economic, and political life tends to make you attach to certain things.

It is not easy to break these attachments and exercise detachment, but it is possible if one has a strong will and disciplined thinking. Dance can help us destroy such patterns and let the natural patterns reveal themselves.

Attachment brings fear, anger, hatred, and the world conditions in which we are now. Attachments are broken sometimes by those who have integrated and Soul-infused personalities. They can break such formations by certain sounds; by shocking you by hitting your back with their hands; by gazing at you; by making you perform certain movements accompanied with your emotions and thought.

One must also consider that the destruction of the patterns can create certain problems in the aura. The process must be done very slowly until the trash of the old patterns is thrown out of the aura. Many physical, emotional, and mental problems appear if the destruction of crystallized patterns is done at once or in haste.

Detachment from old patterns is not easy, and the attachment to old patterns of sex, property, money, titles, and traditions makes life very painful, especially at the stage when all is going to be taken from your hands. This is why, as the life advances, a conscious detachment must be exercised to free oneself for the flight toward the Higher Worlds.

Absence of artificial patterns is a condition of harmony. The presence of artificial patterns is a threat to your health and sanity. Certain artificial or imposed patterns manifest in the form of certain illnesses. Removal of patterns corrects the condition.

It is also possible that the patterns of the parents are inherited by their children. One day it will even be proven that patterns influence the genes.

Each pattern is related to a mental, emotional, or etheric center and to a gland. Actually, you condition their functioning through your patterns. If the patterns are contradictory to the basic patterns of energy in your system, they create disturbances in these centers and glands.

Your patterns are projected onto other people through your behavior, emotions, thoughts, and words. When they accept your patterns, it creates slavery in them and decreases their power of freedom. If they reject the attacking pattern, it sometimes creates lasting conflicts. This is what life is, and we can say that cleansing of patterns is a service to others.

Patterns form when one does the same thing continuously, feels the same way, imagines and thinks in the same way. The body must have a chance to run, to rest, to do different movements and dances in order not to create any patterns. The emotions must be expanding, more inclusive, aspirational, devotional, compassionate, and kind in order to reestablish the original pattern existing in the aura. The thoughts must not follow imposed ways of thinking, or thinking through conflicting, unconstructive patterns. They must follow a path of expansion of horizons and a path of increasing viewpoints, plus a path of spiral climbing to reach astral and fiery dimensions and measures.

Wherever unfoldment and expansion stop, crystallizations step in and decay starts. When any action, emotion, or thought becomes mechanical and crystallizes, it reverses its own nature and becomes an obstacle. For example, when energy becomes matter or water becomes ice, when prayer turns into habit, when a virtue forces itself — these are examples of reversals. When you lie, you reverse yourself because you are the *truth* in your Real Self. When you hate, you reverse yourself because you are *love* in your true nature. When you do ugly things, you reverse yourself because you are *beauty* in your essence.

Everything that is hindering your being your True Self becomes a crystallized pattern and reverses its nature. For example, love turns into hatred when it crystallizes and limits itself.

A child finished high school. His Father said, "Well, you did well, but it is nothing if you compare your achievement with future greater achievements... " The boy finished college. His Father repeated the same words. The boy finished graduate school. His Father said, "It is nothing if you do not use all your knowledge and talents to help humanity."

His Father was trying to teach him not to crystallize in his knowledge, position, or possessions but to be a flow of energy leading toward greater service. This is exactly what builders do. They build the scaffolding very carefully, and when the building is finished they bring down the scaffolding. But people carry their scaffolding patterns to the end!

People sometimes think that the Plan of the Hierarchy is a set pattern. It is not; it is an ever-growing, changing, adjusting symphony because it is the meeting point of the human need and the Divine Purpose. The Divine Plan does not lead into fixations but toward universalization.

The race develops by presented patterns given by advanced human beings. When man approaches the flower bud of the pattern, he perceives that it is not the bud he saw before. When he approaches the flower of the pattern, the pattern changes into a more complicated configuration. This continues until man finds intuitively the next step of his evolution. Thus patterns are not motels but highways passing continuously through a greater beauty of Mother Nature.

There is a word that is not yet thoroughly explained. That word is *mood*. Esoterically, mood is a certain condition of the aura that is conductive to various emotions and thoughts. Mood controls the glands, the nervous system, the organs, and facial expressions.

To create a mood means to make yourself conductive to certain thoughts or emotions. For example, an actor can cry any time he or she wants, or feel great joy. He has power over his emotional and mental substance and can mold them through any thought or emotion.

One can use this technique of creating moods in various circumstances. For example, before you dance, you create the mood that the dance is for, or you can create devotion, solemnity, serenity, or peace in needed conditions.

The mood transmits the energy you want. Before people engage in any work or service or creativity, they create their mood and amplify it during the performance. Without mood, things will be dry and flat. For example, before you deliver a lecture you must charge yourself with certain moods. Before you play the violin or piano, you must create your mood. Then the mood turns into a channel of inspiration.

The mood is created by imagination, visualization, aspiration, ecstasy, and by willpower. You can use these techniques if you can. Little children can create their mood through imagination very easily.

Before you start with your sacred dance or ceremony, you must create the mood, a mood of withdrawal from the common life, a mood of solemnity, aspiration, contact with the divine; a mood of divine carelessness, joy. After you put yourself in the sphere of such a mood, your performance will be magnetic and radioactive because it will draw higher forces into you.

Chapter 29

Dance of the Seven Rays

Here is a beautiful dance that depicts the Seven Rays, the rainbow, or the seven centers:

1. Seven people compose each Ray and there are seven Rays. We need forty-nine people plus one at the center.

2. Each Ray has its specific color, and the central person is dressed totally in white.

3. The participants, led by the White One, start moving with the music and circle the hall in single file and turn in a circle three times.

4. As they walk again in a circle, each color parts as a Ray forming a circle. At the center stands the White One. From the diagram on the next page you see seven circles, or Seven Rays.

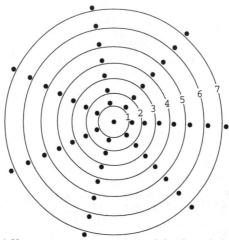

5. All movements start with the right foot. All movements must be graceful. The distances between people must be kept equal so that the circles are circles and the Rays are the same distance from each other.

6. Each Ray has its symbol on the color of the costume. White is the synthesis of all.

7. When the separation of the Rays is being formed, you must walk proportionately faster or slower to fill the distance the forming Rays are creating in the circle.

8. Rays have their numbers. The First Ray is number one; the Seventh Ray is number seven. The number one must turn clockwise, the number two counterclockwise, and so on, and in one revolution they must come to the color of their own Ray.

9. The turning must be so rhythmic and harmonious that various colors will blend and eventually separate again in the rhythmic music.

10. You will note that to keep pace, the outer circle must move faster, the innermost circle the slowest.

The color combinations are a delight for the Devas who enjoy such ceremonial dances very much and pour their blessings on the dancers and the audience.[1]

11. The separation of the circle into Rays, or colors, must be arranged wisely so that the circle disappears into the seven circles, or Seven Rays.

12. On the floor you must have seven marks for the distribution of the Seven Rays. Always the First one goes toward the center.

13. The separation of the circle into Rays is not easy. Extreme discipline and concentration must be exercised to do it perfectly, but it is the concentration and discipline that creates the needed magnetism to draw higher energies to the participants.

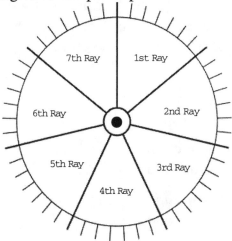

1. See the *Aura, Shield of Protection & Glory* for colors of the Rays.

Music and Chanting

At the first movement, the center person says,

The Lord of the seven powers of the Universe,
inspire me with Your purpose.

Turning clockwise in place with raised hands and arms, he keeps his location so that he does not move out of his position.

When the center person starts the invocation, the first circle moves, then the second moves, the third moves, and so on, but all are synchronized in such a way that the invocation and the movement of each circle coordinate with the others.

The center person is chanting the invocation very slowly in the note D.

The center person is invoking and the circles are absorbing the energy and distributing it into space.

When one revolution is done around the center and all are back in their proper places they say, while standing still,

May the inspiration reach us, and enlighten
our whole being.

This must be chanted on the note C.

At the second move the Center says,

May the inspiration reach you, enlighten you,
and radiate out to the worlds of men.

The second move is in a circle as you did before, and when you are in your proper places and the Center's invocation is over, you say,

> *May gratitude, joy, and ecstasy, like the fragrance of our souls, rise toward You, O Lord of the Universe.*

Say this in ecstasy and concentration.
At the third move, the Center kneels, and then each Ray kneels one after the other in rhythm and harmony. Then the Center says,

> *May the purpose of our being translate itself into the Plan in our souls. May we see in the light our path to follow.*

After this invocation the Rays raise up their hands and bend their heads and say,

> *May we be builders of the Plan and carry upon our shoulders the responsibility of the Service.*

Immediately when this invocation is over, the Center will sound a long OM like a base until the short seven OMs of the Seven Rays are over.

Then the Rays individually, each Ray as a group, will say OM consecutively, one after the other. The note for the Center will be G.

For the Rays, use B,B,D,D,F,F,G.

After the Seventh Ray OM is said, all dancers will sound the OM in the same sound as the note of the Center — G. Here, all dancers stand: first the Center, then each Ray harmoniously. The ideal is: number one starts rising, number two follows, number three follows number two, and so on, each color individually, starting with the far end.[2]

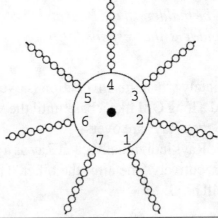

2. Rays 1, 2 sound B; Rays 3, 4 sound D, Rays 5, 6 sound F, Ray 7 sounds G again and all together repeatedly.

The power is in synchronization. Time and motion release energy.

If the heights of dancers are arranged correctly, the movements will be very beautiful. The taller ones will be further from the Center, and each circle will have the same height. The Center will be the tallest.

The Center can be male or female. The colors will start male or female according to the gender of the Center. If the Center is male, the first circle will be female, then male, female, with the seventh or outermost circle female. If the Center is female, the first circle will be male, then female, with the seventh or outermost circle male.

At the fourth move when all stand, the Center will say,

O Mighty Lord, the King of Peace, may Your Presence be felt in our life so that we translate the Plan through our thoughts, words, and actions.

After the Center speaks, each Ray will say,

Ray 1 — *OM*

Ray 2 — *ma*

Ray 3 — *ni*

Ray 4 — *pad*

Ray 5 — *me*

Ray 6 — *hum*

Ray 7 — *OM*

At the fifth move after a short silence, the Center will say,

O Great Lord, let Your eyes behold us, protect
us, inspire us, lead us.

Immediately when the Center and the Rays complete the statement, the forty-nine members will clap their hands three times, raise their hands to their hearts, and each Ray will say the following, one after the other:

Ray 1 — *O Great Lord,*

Ray 2 — *let Your eyes*

Ray 3 — *behold us,*

Ray 4 — *protect us,*

Ray 5 — *inspire us,*

Ray 6 — *lead us.*

Ray 7 — *OM* (short)

and then all together repeat *OM*

As the forty-nine clap their hands as one, the Center will raise his hand as if in admiration. At the sixth move the Center kneels. The circle closest to the Center then kneels, and so on to the seventh circle. When all are on their knees, they will say with great trust and force,

O Thou Who called us to the path of labor,
accept our ableness and our desire, accept our
labor, O Lord, because by day and by night
Thou beholdest us. Manifest Thy hand, O
Lord, because great is darkness. We follow
Thee.

At the seventh move the Center rises. The next circle rises and so on, until all are standing. Then the Center says,

My Lord, we will carry the Chalice of Labor
on our heads and Your torch in our hearts.

All will turn 360 degrees. The Center clockwise, and the first circle — circle nearest the Center — counterclockwise, and so on. All movements must be done very gracefully and synchronously.

All together will repeat:

Joy to earth and to heavens. Peace to earth
and to heavens.

Then the Center will sound the OM on the note G.

All will respond in unison:

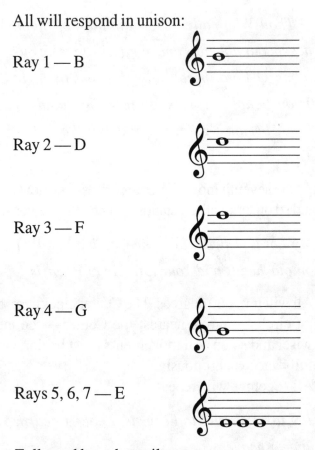

Ray 1 — B

Ray 2 — D

Ray 3 — F

Ray 4 — G

Rays 5, 6, 7 — E

Followed by a deep silence.

The Center will go and take from the altar fifty candles and stand outside of the circles.

Each Ray will withdraw backward to the farthest circle, and the farthest circle will expand as one by one it receives the Rays into its circle.

When the circle is formed, they will walk in a circle three times, and as each member passes by the Center, the Center will give each a lighted candle and they all will walk in the circle with the candles. The Center is the Leader. After the third encirclement they will walk out singing *Om Mani Padme Hum.*[3]

---

3. This mantram can be found on the tape *Go in Beauty*, which can be ordered from the publisher.

Chapter 30

Why Singing

When people sing, the following effects are produced within them:

1. The atoms of all the bodies are rearranged in certain patterns that are either beneficial or harmful.

2. Many hidden, suppressed emotions are expressed, thereby increasing or decreasing the vitality of the body.

3. Many "dead" atoms are thrown out of the aura.

4. Many glamors and illusions are destroyed or built.

5. Some subconscious elements are brought out into the field of the conscious mind, causing

temporary or lasting disturbances, or there is a great release of inner tensions.

6. Soul-infusion is achieved temporarily or permanently.

7. Higher contacts are achieved with advanced entities in space.

8. The environment is purified or polluted according to the energy expressed through the song.

9. The centers are opened or closed, according to the frequency of the notes used in the songs and according to the level where it is going. Songs may be sung on four levels: physical, astral, mental, and intuitional.

10. Change of chemistry occurs in the glands and organs.

Let us analyze each of these effects:

1. Sound has powerful organizing and disorganizing effects on atoms. Usually, notes tuned in with higher bodies have organizing effects on the atoms of the bodies. Notes tuned in with lower centers or with glamors, maya, and illusions have disturbing and disorganizing effects, especially when the thoughts and negative emotions reinforce these notes.

The organization of notes in higher patterns brings happiness, health, and energy. When patterns are disturbed or disorganized, they bring various health problems. The patterns referred to are geometrical formations of energies, extending from one center to another. For example, a higher pattern is the network of energies formed between the heart, throat, and head centers, and a lower pattern is the formation of forces extending between a glamor, the solar plexus center, and the sacral center.

2. Through our singing, many kinds of hidden and suppressed emotions are released into our aura. If these energies are of higher order, they bring vitality into our body; if of a low order, they bring pollution into our aura.

There are four sounds at our level, and when we sing we use one or two, or three or four of these sounds together. What are these sounds? There is the physical vocal sound, which is the audible sound. Then we have the sound of our emotions, which carries a powerful frequency but is inaudible. This is the sound of our desires, emotions, feelings, wishes, and aspirations. Often, this sound does not support our audible sound, and we have only one agent of impression.

Then we have the sound of our thoughts or thoughtforms. These have a very low frequency and therefore penetrate into the minds of the people and affect them. Sometimes the mental sound is an octave higher than the audible sound. Sometimes it creates a harmonic with the astral and audible notes.

Then we have the sounds of the ether — the sound of our Solar Angel, or our human soul. These sounds bring great changes in those who have ears to hear. These sounds, if present in our voice, create a very powerful and transformative effect in our nature.

The voice of our Soul is transmitted via the *Antahkarana* and through our highest vision, love, and freedom. The voice of our Solar Angel is revelatory. While we sing, the voice of our Solar Angel causes deep revelations within us related to the Universe, to creation, or to our future. These sounds are produced if we purify ourselves and build our *Antahkarana.*

Those who sing while physically in maya, emotionally in glamor, and mentally in illusion can sing, but their voice is not pure and in harmony with the pure notes, and they carry pollution to those who hear them. True singers are those who assist the Creator to continue His creative labor.

The speeches of Great Ones are like songs, and Their words are charged with the harmonics of the four notes, thus charging the notes of their physical sound.

3. Our singing can throw away "dead" atoms from our aura. When sound is pure and linked with higher sounds, it becomes an instrument of purification in all our bodies. Our health improves and our energy increases as we sing. We see a clarity in our thinking, a purity in our feelings and emotions, and a coordinative freedom in all our actions.

4. Singing can destroy not only our glamors and illusions, but it may also build new glamors and illusions.

Destruction of glamors takes place if the sound of
the human soul is within your voice. The illusions are
destroyed if the sound of the Solar Angel or the Intuition is active in your voice. The purification of glamors
and illusions brings to you a tremendous current of energy from the Higher Worlds. This energy integrates
and transforms a group and can be used to purify a
nation or humanity.

But if your song or voice is related to jealousy,
hatred, fear, anger, revenge, slander, lust, or greed, as
you sing, you increase your glamors and illusions or
build new ones.

5. The subconscious elements are drawn out into
the field of your conscious mind, causing temporary or
lasting disturbances or a great release of the inner tension.

Often the release of subconscious elements creates crises in our life, and we feel flooded by unfamiliar
or strong urges and drives. Sometimes we lose control
over our actions, emotions, thoughts, and words, em-
barrassing ourselves and others. Such disturbances
evaporate in the light of our Higher Self or root themselves in the conscious mind and in the emotional body
if they link themselves with our glamors, illusions, and
maya.

It is important to know that sound burns the protect-
ing wall of the subconscious and releases certain tensions.
Such a release takes place if the song is inspired by higher
visions and higher revelations. The fire of such visions

and revelations burns away the subconscious elements. Indirectly they are released.

This is also done through music. When an advanced artist plays music on a violin or piano or on any instrument, it is possible that the inaudible notes of the emotions, mind, human soul, and Solar Angel synchronize with the audible notes and create a tremendous effect on the audience. These are the secrets of those who are musical geniuses.

One day my Mother, after listening to a girl singing a mantram, whispered in my ear, "Do you hear the voice of her Angel in her voice?" I opened my eyes wide and looked at my Mother in great surprise. She repeated the question and I whispered, "I hear her song through both of my ears and also my heart." She did not answer, but I saw tear drops coming from her eyes.

You can have such an experience if you learn to listen with different centers in your body.

6. Singing helps you to achieve temporary or permanent Soul-infusion. This happens when your Solar Angel sings with you to transform those who hear your voice. This can be a very uplifting experience. You stand above your sorrows and personality problems and see life from an infinite viewpoint. It is often in these moments that great currents of inspiration fill your being for highly creative labor.

7. Higher contacts are achieved with advanced entities in space. Higher entities love the colors emanated from your songs. They contact you as a gratitude

for your offerings or to lead you to higher services. If you read many traditions, you will see that the voice is used in singing, chanting, and praying to contact higher realms.

Sound opens the channels leading to the Higher Worlds. It is as if a beam of light pierces the clouds and smog and reaches the earth. Sound destroys obstacles or repulses accumulated hindrances to bridge the person with the Higher Worlds.

8. Our environment is purified or polluted according to the energy expressed through our song or music.

Our thoughts, conversations, emotions, and actions stick to the walls and furniture. Sometimes a wall is loaded with thousands of thoughtforms. Sometimes our furniture and carpets are soaked by our thoughts and emotions. Sometimes all the ceiling and floors are ornamented by our beautiful emotions, or they stink because of the emotions of our lust, hatred, crimes, etc.

In the old days when a new building was erected or a new home was bought, the owners used to bring holy men or women to bless their home through singing and mantrams or chanting. This is a very scientific procedure to destroy negative accumulations and create a pure atmosphere for the dwellers. Of course, new or old homes are polluted by songs or speech coming from glamors, illusions, maya, lust, hatred, revenge, or from darker sources.

Some Temples do not allow a person to enter unless he is initiated or purified.

9. Our voice, sounds, and conversations can nourish our centers if they are of high quality. Sound is the nourishment of the flowers. You can kill flowers by noises or conversations that carry malice and hatred.

Many times after singing, playing music, or talking we feel empty and blocked. The reason is that the quality of our voice closed certain centers in our bodies.

10. The chemistry of our centers, organs, and glands changes because of our voice, singing, or talking. Chemistry is the result of atomic arrangement. It is the frequency of our voice that rearranges, changes, or creates new chemistry within our body.

In the future, healing of the bodies will take place through sound and singing. A chart will be prepared on which will be shown the chemical elements and their corresponding notes. Healers will be composers of special songs or music which will create certain chemicals for our organs, emotional, or mental bodies. Or they will create songs or music to eliminate certain chemicals from these bodies.

Thus, the man will learn to be his own creator because his voice will reverberate with the sound of the Will of the Creator.

Chapter 31

How to Sing

In teaching how to sing, some teachers make their students practice imitating the voices of animals such as a cat, dog, wolf, horse. We are told that such animal imitations disturb the nadis (etheric nerve system), cut communication with the Higher Self, and invite animal magnetism to people. They coarsen the consciousness and eventually affect the vocal cords.

Songs must be sung gradually through higher planes. For example, you may sing as a body, as emotions, as mind, and as a soul. Physical songs are concrete, objective. Emotional songs have aspiration, hate, love, fear, and so on. Mental songs are precise; they have meaning, direction, architecture, and so on. Soul songs have motive, future, eternity, and so on.

306 The Creative Sound

It is not easy to discriminate these levels, but as one continues singing, suddenly he realizes that he is singing through various levels. After having certain experiences one can rehearse until he is familiar with the various levels and sings at that level when he wants or as the condition requires.

The words of songs also are written on one of these four levels. There are words or sentences that are physical, emotional, mental, or spiritual. Generally, the words control the level on which you want to sing.

It is the level that determines the kind and voltage of energy you transmit to your audience. Often, the words are hopeless, but it is the tonality that affects and the tonality reflects the level of the consciousness of the person who is singing.

During singing one can raise his level or be a clear transmitter of a certain level if he learns to sing with visualization. A person only singing the word "rose" will have a different influence than one who visualizes the rose as he sings. Some great singers are also very trained in visualization techniques.

In rehearsal it is good to exercise by using letters of an alphabet, not only English but many other languages as well. Different alphabets have different power and different notes. It is good also to form short syllables and sing them on four levels with visualization.

We had a Teacher who used to make us sing using colors. We used to visualize colors as we were singing the given note. This is a very powerful psychological exercise which can highly prepare the singers.

It is also possible to take symbols, visualize them, and sing them. You will be surprised what a different tonality you will have with different, simple symbols, for example, triangles, squares, circles, and so on.

The important issue is that the singer must have access to the sources of higher levels and sources of higher energies, bring them down, and share them with others to uplift and free them from their limitations. The exact purpose of singing is

a. To tap sources of higher energies

b. To transmit higher energies in their purity

c. To uplift people

d. To free people from their limitations

All great singers are liberators.

Chapter 32

Sound and Voice

The sublimation of the sacral center is carried out through our speech and especially through our singing. The throat center and sacral centers are creative centers. The sacral center creates with different matter than the throat center, though they can cooperate and benefit from each other's energy or substance. The throat center acts as a transmitting or sublimating agent for the forces of the sacral center.

Sometimes the sacral center deprives the throat center, wasting the creative energy in lust or in excessive sex. Sometimes the throat center draws so much energy from the sacral center that the latter goes through a time of sleep or inactivity. True celibacy starts from the moment when the sacral center offers its energy to the throat center, which then uses it in creative art, in painting, in writing, and especially in creative lectures or in singing. Singing and chanting are the best means to use the sacral energy for creative labor.

Often it happens that those who are not yet sublimated in their sex center get stimulated by the singing or speech of advanced people and fall in love. "Falling in love" is a phenomenon in which the sex center is activated and is in the process of sublimation. Sublimated energies let the subject become strongly attracted to the speaker or the singer. The same process works in Nature. The animals and birds attract their mates especially by their voice and singing.

Voice and singing activate the sacral center and make sexual relationship possible. Later, science will reveal to us how the chemical phenomena are the result of sound, the most creative agent in the Universe.

Of course in the use of sound as in other things, people can misuse it for their selfish and harmful intentions. When sound or singing and speech are used to manipulate people through their sex or throat centers, they fall into black magic. We see this in some contemporary music in which death, lust, and horror are advertised. Such songs and music can, for a long time, seal the throat center and stop the evolution of people.

If singing is used to inflame lust, hatred, fear, and so on, it damages the throat center and draws the fire from the sacral center without causing transmutation in that fire.

Simply stated, we have throat center energy, we have sacral center energy, and we have the necessity to sublimate sex energy. Sublimation of sex energy occurs when the throat center energy is charged with high or lofty thought, visions, principles, and beauty. It is in this charge that sublimation takes place. But if the sacral center fire is drawn up by creative activities without the process of sublimation, it pollutes the throat energy or throat center, and it eventually manifests as various kinds of diseases.

This is also true with our speech. Speech can transmute sacral center fire if it is charged with truth, fact, and with higher ideas and so on. But if our speech is loaded with gossip, destruction, criticism, slander, malice, hatred, or our conversation is not on a high level, the transmutation does not occur.

The chemistry of the voice of a real male and of a real female is very different. The female voice is more attractive, synthesizing, loving, invoking, and magnetic. The male voice is stimulative, positive, evoking, expanding, radioactive, and demanding. But in this age, real types of male and female voices are getting more and more rare. The voices and sound are losing their pure characteristics. Listen to the voice of your Mother, especially when she expresses her admiration and love to you. And listen to the voice of your Father when he tries to give guidance and encouragement to you in your striving. It is all energy phenomena.

This is also true in Nature's phenomena, such as the sounds of forests, rivers, oceans, winds, eruptions of volcanic mountains. Many sounds can have very astonishing effects on our life and direction. We can experience this in voices or sounds coming from astral, mental, and higher planes. One of my friends changed his whole life when he heard his Master's voice calling him for a great service and sacrifice. You can find such experiences in the history of every nation.

In subjective words or calls you can also find duality those calls that pave the way for your spiritual evolution and those calls that push you into the mud of life. You must learn how to discriminate.

It is very evident that the integrity of nations falls or rises according to the use of the voice and sound or speech. Those who misuse the creative energy with their songs and speeches, with lies and fabrications, to gain superiority and control or to mislead people pay a severe taxation, even inviting the reactions of Nature in forms of cataclysms.

A legend says that Great Ones listen to the collective sounds of persons, groups, and nations and see their future. Progress in the coming age will be signaled by those who use their voice and sound goal-fittingly and develop their power of discrimination to choose the path of sublimation and transformation.

Chapter 33

The Mystery of Hearing

Hearing is of four kinds. The first one is the ordinary hearing with our physical ears. Many people not only have hearing problems but also do not have the power of attention and the understanding of what they hear.

The second one is astral hearing. This is when one hears the conversations of astral entities or translates the words and sentences into astral sound.

The third is mental hearing. This is when one can hear and remember many conversations going on in the mental plane.

All of our thinking is conversation on the mental plane. In special groups and conversations, we pass information to each other. All these conversations are possible to hear, or all dialogue going on in thinking can be translated on the physical plane as sound if the mental sense of hearing is developed.

The fourth hearing is called real hearing; it is hearing of intuitional sound. Those who attend classes in their sleep often forget any conversation or Teaching given to them on this plane. Few people can hear intuitionally and remember. Also, only a very small number of people can hear Intuitional Plane talk with their physical ears. Christ gave many proofs of this.

In the history of humanity there are many who had clairaudience on all these planes.

One of the senses that must be developed is subjective and objective hearing. It is important that our physical, emotional, mental, and intuitional ears coordinate with each other so that we are able to hear and remember all that we need to hear from these planes, especially when our Teacher is to impart needed instructions to us. Many profound unfoldments of our consciousness are caused by hearing and remembering our Teacher's instructions.

It is not necessary to sleep to hear your Teacher's voice. You can hear it in your daily occupations as He is instructing those who are subjectively with Him. You can hear His voice during your meditation, prayer, and sleep.

But the Teachers are very cautious about talking to you during meditation because the dark forces do the same thing when you fall into the astral plane. This is why, except on special occasions, They impress your mind during your meditation with certain lofty ideas.

In the West no one is interested in cultivating his hearing on all four planes. But in some Far Eastern countries this is a part of the spiritual discipline.

The steps are as follows:

1. Avoid noise and, as much as possible, disharmony and shocking sounds.

2. Do not listen to conversations that are ugly, loud, emotional, hurtful, and so on.

3. Speak very softly.

4. Listen to good music.

5. Practice listening to a friend's conversation at a given time when he will "call" you and say a few words subjectively. This is an exercise that must be done everyday for years until the result is seen and you are able to hear his real voice and talk back to him.

6. Try to hear your Solar Angel's voice after asking an important question.

7. Try to hear the voice of your Master at the exact time of the Full Moon.

If you do all these very faithfully, soon you will see results.

Before you try to hear on any level, dedicate yourself to Christ and focus your mind at the top of your head, in the Light of your Soul. This will protect you from hearing the voices of dark forces and astral entities.

No matter how little you do these exercises, they can have a good effect on your hearing, and if you succeed, keep it highly confidential. Higher powers, when actualized, must be kept secret, as when one has diamonds and keeps it a secret. Talking about your psychic powers leads you toward destruction. It is the beauty of your life that must lead people, not your boasting or showing off, which creates a reverse effect on your life.

You need to have these powers only to be able to render better service to humanity for its spiritual development.

Chapter 34

Ceremonies, Rituals, and Sacraments in the Future

Ceremonies, rituals, and sacraments are three sides of a triangle. These three go together when we are engaged in making a higher contact, in the process of receiving and assimilating energy, and in the task of distribution of energy.

A *sacrament* is the contact point with a source of energy, which can be an idea, a vision, a focus of energy rays, or a center such as the Hierarchy, Shamballa, even a sun, a zodiac, or the innermost Self within a person. It is the point of inspiration.

Rituals are the methods, the scientific techniques or formulas used to receive, to accumulate, to transform these energies, and to adapt them to the need of the masses. Rituals cause enlightenment. They build the bridge between the masses and the source of energy or the divine contact.

Ceremonies are the ways and means for assimilation and distribution of these energies, by which the consciousness of the masses is expanded and life is transformed or sublimated. Ceremonies build the bridge between the masses and rituals. They are related to human beings, to their centers, to their emotions, thoughts, and relations with other people. Ceremonies are the ways and means by which to protect the incoming energy through right assimilation and right distribution. Thus, ceremonies protect the masses from overstimulation and help them to assimilate the charge released by the rituals.

Ceremonies, if they are scientifically organized, create alignment and integration within the three lower vehicles: physical-etheric, emotional, and mental. They create a new relationship between the centers below and above the diaphragm; they expand the vision and receptivity of the masses; and they shield them from negative influences by creating a field of powerful radiation.

In the past, people looked at these processes as religious practices based on faith and worship. In the future we will come to the realization that sacraments, rituals, and ceremonies are scientific formulas of service and subtle mechanisms of contact. This mechanism of contact has an actual existence. It is built of etheric, emotional, and mental energies that are galvanized by love, intelligence, and will, ensouled with a purpose, and manifested as organized and creative actions and movements. This mechanism exists to

* evoke energy
* absorb energy
* transmit energy

The service in the future will be a bridging process between the highest and lowest. This mechanism of sacrament, ritual, and ceremony is the fulcrum of the science of true service. The contacted energies can be used for transmutation, transformation, and transfiguration, gradually raising the awareness unit of the unfolding human soul to higher levels of reality.

As our consciousness expands and contacts higher levels of reality, we gain control, proportionately, over our vehicles of manifestation and their associated activities. These formulas of service are carried out by three ranks of people.

1. An *individual* (or an integrated group) who officiates. This is the celebrant, who is the contact point with the energy center. Usually this is handled by an Initiate of the Mysteries, or by a Knower, through contemplation or *samadhi*.

2. A *group* of highly developed people, who are able to perform the rituals and to receive, assimilate, and transmit the energy. Usually these are disciples. This group uses occult, scientific meditation.

3. The *masses* of people, who are receptive to the incoming energy and distribute it in their contacts. Such masses represent the aspirants of the world. This large group uses invocation, prayer, and chanting, plus their minds and emotions.

Sacraments are related to great Avatars, devas, angels, or to great energy centers in the planet or in the solar system. In sacraments, the willpower in the Spiritual Triad is used through the life thread or sutratma. The sacrament corresponds to Purpose.

Rituals are related to the energy of love, of the heart, to the Intuition, to the soul, to the Antahkarana, and to thought. Rituals are arranged according to the principles of rhythm and cycles and are based on solar, zodiacal, and various astrological configurations. Through the ritual, the soul of the public is connected to the source of power. Ritual corresponds to the Divine Plan.

Ceremonies create receptivity and sensitivity in the participants, and they are related to the public or to the aspirants of the world in any branch of human endeavor. In ceremony the creative thread is used. Ceremony corresponds to labor, which works out the Plan inspired by the Purpose.

There exist patterns of activities of divine principles, laws, and energies, patterns of activities of spiritual entities or centers. All these activities exist as a mechanism of solar or universal contact, as a mechanism to supply energy and guidance to lower strata of existence, and to provide a bridge for unfoldment and expansion. Sacraments, rituals, and ceremonies are symbolic reflections and allegorical teachings of those patterns of activity upon the mental subplanes of advanced human beings. These beings then formulate and organize them in order to provide for humanity a path of enlightenment, healing, group work, sacrificial service, and synchronization with the rhythm and cycles of Cosmos.

Thus a sacrament, a ritual, a ceremony has its own symbols that are links between the divine, subjective activities and human striving and labor.

A *symbol* is a pattern of energy flow. If it is used correctly, it transfers energy of certain kinds that can be used in harmony with subjective activities. The energy of symbols can be released in various intensities through

- eye contact
- devotion, admiration, worship
- contact, thinking, and meditation
- the Intuition
- identification in contemplation

A symbol can be used more effectively if the one who makes contact has, in his nature, an element of substance that corresponds to the substance of the originating source of the symbol.

There are, for example, fundamental mental symbols, such as the sphere, the pyramid, the triangle, the cross, the fire, the five-pointed star, the Chalice, the rod, stones,

colors, musical notes, words, and signs of power. All these
are like tuning forks that evoke responses from the centers of initiates, disciples, and aspirants in various intensities and depths. They also evoke responses from higher
realms within man and Nature.

In *sacraments* the higher centers are used: the head
center, the heart center, the Chalice or the twelve-petaled lotus on the mental plane, and the Spiritual Triad.
A sacrament is a moment of contact with an energy
source in which the celebrant goes through a process of
transfiguration, or at least a high degree of purification.
In such a state of upliftment and polarization, he becomes the recipient of energy, of bliss, of light, of beauty,
of love.

The *ritual* is the mechanism by which to carry
down these virtues through certain stones, metals, incense, oils, bread, wine, water, fire, bells, signs, symbols, and by the signs and words of power. The centers
used in the ritual are mostly throat, heart, and ajna centers, or the eyes.

In *ceremonies*, it is mostly motions, movements,
rhythm, cycles, symbols, colors, and chants that are
used to draw down the energy from the ritual and spread
it to the members and participants.

A ritual is a great living symbol that carries within
its heart the purpose of the sacrament and adapts it to
the need of the masses. Thus, the purpose changes into
a plan through which the purpose can work itself out.

In ceremony, the Purpose and the Plan are symbolized in such a way that those who have eyes to *see* and even those who are not awake enough can still benefit from the energy the symbolic ceremony releases. Through ceremony, the masses of people have an opportunity to contact the spiritual nature within each other. Such a contact results in the power of discrimination, a sense of responsibility, and group consciousness.

Ceremonies must be arranged in such a way that they reflect the vision of the sacrament. Those who know must carefully arrange the music, the symbols, the movements, the colors, the robes, and the chants in such a way that a unified force field is created with great magnetism. Any wrong arrangement of color, movement, rhythm, chanting, symbols, etc. causes disturbances in the force field created by the symphony of the ceremony.

Participants of ceremonies must be very careful to have right polarization toward greater values, or the ceremony may increase their vices and lower tendencies. We are told that the Intelligence behind our planet, behind our solar system, even behind our galaxy uses these three techniques of contact:

a. Sacrament

b. Ritual

c. Ceremony

It is a *sacrament* when a life contacts a greater life. It is a *ritual* when the energy released through this contact is assimilated and transferred to a lower plane. It is *ceremony* when the released and appropriated energy is finally received by life forms.

The sacraments, the rituals, and the ceremonies of Nature are manifested in the expression of cycles, rhythms, pulses, movements, colors, and sounds of all forms of Nature. The Sun is the sacrament for our solar system. The ritual is the energy interchange between the Sun and our planetary living forms. The ceremony is the process of assimilation and utilization of this energy in all kingdoms and in all forms.

Ceremonies remain in the memory of the people, act as seed thoughts that gradually unfold and unveil the plan and purpose behind the ceremony, and lead the people toward greater understanding of reality. For example, the sacrament of Holy Communion is a central energy focus, the mystic presence of Christ.

The officiant stands in the presence in contemplation, in focused will, and is in a process of fusion with Him to receive Him, to assimilate Him, to contain Him. The ritual, which is carried on through various words and signs of power, meditation, visualization, and chanting, is a supreme mechanism by which to link Him with the heart of the participants.

Ceremony is the distribution of Christ-energy to the public. Thus the purpose, the unity, and the presence in the sacrament reveal themselves in the ritual as an act of sacrifice. In ceremony, the act of sacrifice is translated as the sacrificial service for humanity, which carries into fulfillment the purpose of alignment, integration, and eventual unity.

In the sacrament, the officiant is the Christ within the heart of the celebrant. In the ritual, the officiant is the soul of the transformed priest. In the ceremony, the recipient is the transformed heart of the public who receives the communion and becomes group conscious.

Ceremonial rituals may be formulated into seven forms, according to the seven main streams of energy, or Seven Rays.

1. The First Ray ritual provides those conditions that create either synthesis or destruction to those forms that prevent the expansion of the inner life.

Such a ritual will manifest itself through a ceremony that will unite the little wills of men and fuse them with a Greater Will to achieve synthesis, or it will annihilate the obstacles to expansion. First Ray ritual uses mostly precious stones, minerals, light, and fire. In the First Ray ritual, will energy is used.

2. The Second Ray ritual is for communion or communication with the Transpersonal Self in man or with the Hierarchical Center on the planet and its core the Christ.

Such a ritual is performed to provide those energies and forces that through a ceremony will expand the consciousness of the masses, increase their love and wisdom, and lead them into a life of sacrificial service, which will express itself in the art of healing within the subtle bodies of man. A Second Ray ritual uses mostly incense and flowers. In the Second Ray ritual, the energy of love is used.

3.   In the Third Ray ritual, the energy of the intelligence is used. The Third Ray ritual provides the energy for creativity. Such a ritual provides a condition or energy field within which officiants come into contact with the prototypes, with the blueprints, with the subtle design behind the manifested Universe. The ceremony related to such a ritual is a creative expression of these blueprints through philosophical ideas, thought, and visions and eventually leads to the illumination and transfiguration of the whole man.

4.   The Fourth Ray ritual invokes and evokes those energies that will manifest through the related ceremony as beauty. Beauty is the expression of contact between spirit and matter, brought together by a living idea. Such a ceremony spreads the sense of beauty: beauty of sound, beauty of color, beauty of movement, beauty in relationships. Harmony is the keynote of such a ceremony.

5.   The Fifth Ray ritual provides those energies that with help man contact the principles, laws, and energies behind the manifested Universe. He can then use them through certain ceremonies to stimulate the spirit of research, the spirit of accuracy, and the spirit of divine detachment.

6.   The Sixth Ray ritual provides those energies which will uplift the heart and connect it with the sphere of the Intuition. Ceremonies carry these energies to the

masses, opening in them the spirit of worship, admiration, aspiration, idealism, and vision. Most church rituals and ceremonies are of this kind.

7. The Seventh Ray ritual provides those energies that fuse the matter with the spirit, the soul with the body. This will provide the right conditions in which the true ceremonial magic will make its appearance and will provide true vehicles for the manifestations. The ritual of the Seventh Ray will bring down those energies which will make the white magician understand the true power of electricity, water, air, and the atoms of the astral plane. The related ceremony of such a ritual will help the masses to materialize a vision and will urge them toward synthesis, sacrificial service, and the brotherhood of humanity.

We are told that the seven main Ashrams of the Hierarchy have their special rituals and ceremonies, which are scientific formulas and actions used to work with Their own Rays and energies within the corresponding fields. We are told that all Their rituals and ceremonies are for bringing the Plan into manifestation through the seven fields of human endeavor: politics, education, philosophy, the arts, science, religion, and economics.

Those who participate in the labor of rituals must have the following qualities:

a. Purity in all their personality vehicles and in their mental, emotional, and physical natures

b. The ability to lift their heart, expand their consciousness into the sphere of the Spiritual Triad, and remain awake

c. The ability to maintain that high-level vibration or frequency from the beginning to the end of the ritual, thus forming a channel of pure transmission, knowing that energy follows thought

These are the safeguards of the officiant or the celebrant.

The public must also be prepared for the ceremonies. Before they engage in the ceremony, they must purify their bodies. They must fill their hearts with love and compassion. They must purify their mental bodies from negative, disturbing thoughts and make the whole of their mechanisms sensitive to the impressions coming through the ritual.

When we are engaged in rituals and ceremonies, we are literally within a sphere of fire where we invoke and release tremendous amounts of energy. These energies may cause great mental, emotional, physical, and social damage if not properly received, used, and transmitted. The ceremony, the ritual, and communicating with the sacrament may cause serious problems if the contents of the minds and hearts of the participants are not totally in tune with the keynote of the presented sacrament.

Contact with higher voltage energies increases the weeds in our nature if they exist there. Pride, vices, the will-to-rule, glamors, and illusions of various kinds increase in our nature. This is the reason why, in sacred brotherhoods and even in the early church, people were admitted into the ceremonies only after long years of preparation and testing.

The energies contacted have various effects on us according to the content of our nature, the elements our nature has built, and the level of our evolution. If we are attached to wrong ways and harmful thinking; if we are identified with our negative emotions; if as a result of such conditions our etheric centers show the signs of disturbances; and if we do not have in our souls a firm and strong intent to purify ourselves, then the sacraments, rituals, and ceremonies will give negative results by increasing our vices and lead us into shameful activities. This is why, for example, the church has put so much emphasis upon confession. Confession was the first conscious step toward the right intent and the right decision to purify and make oneself ready for participation in the sacraments.

Often the officiant or the celebrant, due to his unclean aura or radiations, pollutes the energy contacted by the ritual and transfers that energy to the participants. This can happen if he does not have perfect control over his mental-emotional body. Any degenerate thought or emotion can create disturbances and pollutions within the system of the transmitted energies and cause frictions, reactions, and disturbances within the etheric centers of the participants. This is why the celebrant is expected to be a pure transmitter or an Initiate. The New Era, the Aquarian Age, will create its own sacraments and its own rituals and ceremonies based on the idea of world service, one humanity, and the transformation of the planet. Such rituals and ceremonies will not crystallize the flow of energy into dogmas and doctrines but will keep open the channel between the human soul and the Source of inspiration, so that those who are on their path of spiritual striving may unfold and bloom without impositions and pressures from man-made formulas.

Let us also be mindful that rituals and ceremonies lose their creative influence on people and become merely empty shells when they are performed mechanically, without a conscious striving for the expansion of awareness and for the deepening of experience. Regular performance of the same ritual and ceremony may eventually turn into a habit, and people mistake that mechanical performance for the guarantee of their spiritual security, their progress, and even their salvation. For such people, rituals and ceremonies are hindrances on the path of their intellectual and spiritual progress, making them slaves of mere form.

In order to avoid such a danger we must cultivate conscious, enthusiastic participation, and we must steadily strive to expand our consciousness on higher levels of existence at the time we are engaged in rituals and ceremonies. Rituals and ceremonies become mechanical if we always approach them with the same level of consciousness. It is the expansion of our consciousness and the transmutation of our natures that make a ritual and ceremony ever new for us and a source of ever-flowering inspiration. Greater occultists, greater artists, and greater White Magicians will reappear to show us once again the way to the Central Spiritual Sun.

Index

About the Author

Torkom Saraydarian (1917 – 1997) was born in Asia Minor. Since childhood he was trained in the Teachings of the Ageless Wisdom.

He visited monasteries, ancient temples, and mystery schools in order to find the answers to his questions about the mystery of man and the Universe.

He lived with Sufis, dervishes, Christian mystics, and masters of temple music and dance. His musical training included the violin, piano, oud, cello, and guitar. It took long years of discipline and sacrifice to absorb the Ageless Wisdom from its true sources. Meditation became a part of his daily life, and service a natural expression of his soul.

Torkom Saraydarian dedicated his entire life to the service of his fellow man. His writings and lectures and music show his total devotion to the higher principles, values, and laws that are present in all world religions and philosophies. These works represent a synthesis of the best and most beautiful in the sacred culture of the world. His works enrich the foundational thinking on which man can construct his Future.

Torkom Saraydarian wrote a large number of books, many of which have been published. All of his books will continue to be published and distributed. A few have been translated into Armenian, German, Italian, Spanish, Portuguese, Greek, Dutch, and Danish.

He left a rich legacy of writings and musical compositions for all of humanity to enjoy and benefit from for many years to come.

Visit our web site at *www.tsg-publishing.com* for interviews and additional information on Torkom Saraydarian.

Other Books by Torkom Saraydarian

- The Ageless Wisdom
- The Aura
- Battling Dark Forces
- The Bhagavad Gita
- Breakthrough to Higher Psychism
- Buddha Sutra — A Dialogue with the Glorious One
- Challenge for Discipleship
- Christ, The Avatar of Sacrificial Love
- A Commentary on Psychic Energy
- Cosmic Shocks
- Cosmos in Man
- The Creative Fire
- Dynamics of Success
- Education as Transformation, Vol. I
- Education as Transformation, Vol. II
- The Eyes of Hierarchy—How the Masters Watch and Help Us
- Flame of Beauty, Culture, Love, Joy
- The Flame of the Heart
- From My Heart — Volume I (Poetry)
- Hiawatha and the Great Peace
- The Hidden Glory of the Inner Man
- I Was
- Joy and Healing
- Karma and Reincarnation
- Leadership Vol. I
- Leadership Vol. II
- Leadership Vol. III
- Leadership Vol. IV
- Leadership Vol. V
- Legend of Shamballa

- The Mystery of Self-Image
- The Mysteries of Willpower
- New Dimensions in Healing
- Olympus World Report... The Year 3000
- One Hundred Names of God
- Other Worlds
- The Psyche and Psychism
- The Psychology of Cooperation and Group Consciousness
- The Purpose of Life
- The Science of Becoming Oneself
- The Science of Meditation
- The Sense of Responsibility in Society
- Sex, Family, and the Woman in Society
- The Solar Angel
- Spiritual Regeneration
- Spring of Prosperity
- The Subconscious Mind and the Chalice
- Symphony of the Zodiac
- Talks on Agni
- Thought & the Glory of Thinking
- Triangles of Fire
- Unusual Court
- Woman, Torch of the Future
- The Year 2000 & After

Booklets
- The Art of Visualization — Simply Presented

- The Chalice in Agni Yoga Literature
- Cornerstones of Health
- A Daily Discipline of Worship
- Discipleship in Action
- Duties of Grandparents
- Earrings for Business People
- Earthquakes and Disasters — What the Ageless Wisdom Tells Us
- Fiery Carriage and Drugs
- Five Great Mantrams of the New Age
- Hierarchy and the Plan
- How to Find Your Level of Meditation
- Inner Blooming
- Irritation — The Destructive Fire
- Mental Exercises
- Nachiketas
- New Beginnings
- Practical Spirituality
- Questioning Traveler and Karma
- Saint Sergius
- Synthesis

Booklets
(Excerpts and Compilations)
- Angels and Devas
- Building Family Unity
- Courage
- Daily Spiritual Striving
- First Steps Toward Freedom
- Prayers, Mantrams, and Invocations
- The Psychology of Cooperation

- Responsibility
- Responsibility and Business
- Responsibilities of Fathers
- Responsibilities of Mothers
  Success
- Torchbearers
- What to Look for in the Heart of Your Partner

Videos
- The Seven Rays Interpreted
- Why Drugs Are Dangerous
- Lecture Videos by Author (list available)

Music
- A Touch of Heart (CD only)
- Dance of the Zodiac
- Far Horizons
- Fire Blossom
- Go In Beauty (songs by Torkom Saraydarian sung by choir)
- Infinity
- Lao Tse
- Light Years Ahead
- Lily in Tibet
- Misty Mountain
- Piano Composition
- Rainbow
- Spirit of My Heart
- Sun Rhythms
- Tears of My Joy
- Toward Freedom
- 1994 Annual Convention Special Edition — Synthesizer Music

About the Publisher

T.S.G. Publishing Foundation, Inc. is a non-profit, tax exempt organization. Founded on November 30, 1987 in Los Angles, California, it relocated to Cave Creek, Arizona on January 1, 1994.

Our purpose is to be a pathway for self-transformation. We are fully devoted to publishing, teaching, and distributing the creative works of Torkom Saraydarian.

Our bookstore in Cave Creek and our online bookstore at our web site *www.tsg-publishing.com* offer the complete collection of the creative works of Torkom Saraydarian for sale and distribution. Our newsletter OUTREACH contains thought-provoking articles excerpted from these books. We also conduct weekly classes, special training seminars, and home study meditation courses.

Coming Soon...

We will be releasing in the near future a book on sacred dance instructions and movements taught by Torkom Saraydarian.

Torkom Saraydarian
Book Publishing Fund

Torkom Saraydarian dedicated his entire life to serving others in their spiritual growth. At the time of his passing, more than 100 manuscripts had been written and prepared for publication. This work represents a seamless tapestry of Wisdom and we are dedicated to publishing the entire collection.

Torkom Saraydarian had the unique wisdom and dedication to write all of these magnificent books in one lifetime. Now it is our turn to do the work. Together we can make his dream a reality and bring his legacy to fruition.

We depend on contributions for the publishing of the books. A special fund, *The Torkom Saraydarian Book Publishing Fund* has been established for the completion of this legacy. Contact us for details about the *Book Fund* and an update regarding remaining manuscripts. You can contribute funds for an entire book, or give any amount you wish on a continuous basis or a one-time contribution.

Your contribution will entitle you to devote an entire book to a loved one, or share the dedication with others in the *Book Fund*.

Thank you for your loving and continuous support.

Participate in the Vision for the Future
Contribute to
The Torkom Saraydarian
Book Publishing Fund

My Pledge:

❏ One-time: $ ____   ❏ Annually: $ ____   ❏ Monthly: $ ____

Name: _____

Address: _____

City / State: _____   Country: _____

Tel #: (   )   – _____

E-mail Address: _____

Method of Payment: ❏ Check/U.S. Money-order   ❏ Visa   ❏MasterCard

Account # _____ – _____ – _____   Exp. date: /

(If using credit card, please include account number & expiration date)

Please send to:
T.S.G. Publishing Foundation, Inc. • Attn: Book Fund
P.O. Box 7068 • Cave Creek, AZ 85327 • U.S.A.
Tel: (480) 502-1909 • Fax: (480) 502-1909
Web site: *www.tsg-publishing.com*
E-mail: *webmaster@tsg-publishing.com*

T.S.G. Publishing Foundation, Inc. is a tax-exempt, non-profit organization.

❏ I would like to pay for the publishing of a book in its entirety.
(Please tell us what you want on the dedication page.)
❏ Please include my name on the list of donors.
❏ No name please, just add this donation to the Book Fund.

Ordering Information

Write to the publisher for additional information regarding:

— Free catalog of author's books and music tapes

— Complete list of lecture tapes and videos
  ($2 postage for each list)

— Placement on mailing list for continuous updates

— A free copy of our newsletter *Outreach*

— **Join our Book Club at no charge. (Receive a 20%
discount with each new release by Torkom Saraydarian. Each
new book is mailed to you automatically as soon as it is
released.) Send us a written approval to include you in the
Book Club.**

Additional copies of *The Creative Sound*
  U.S.$ 25.00

Postage within U.S.A. – $6.00 plus applicable state sales tax
International postage: contact us for surface or air rates.

T.S.G. Publishing Foundation, Inc.
  P.O. Box 7068
  Cave Creek, AZ 85327–7068
  United States of America
  TEL: (480) 502–1909
  FAX: (480) 502–0713
  E-Mail: webmaster@tsg-publishing.com
  Web-site: www.tsg-publishing.com